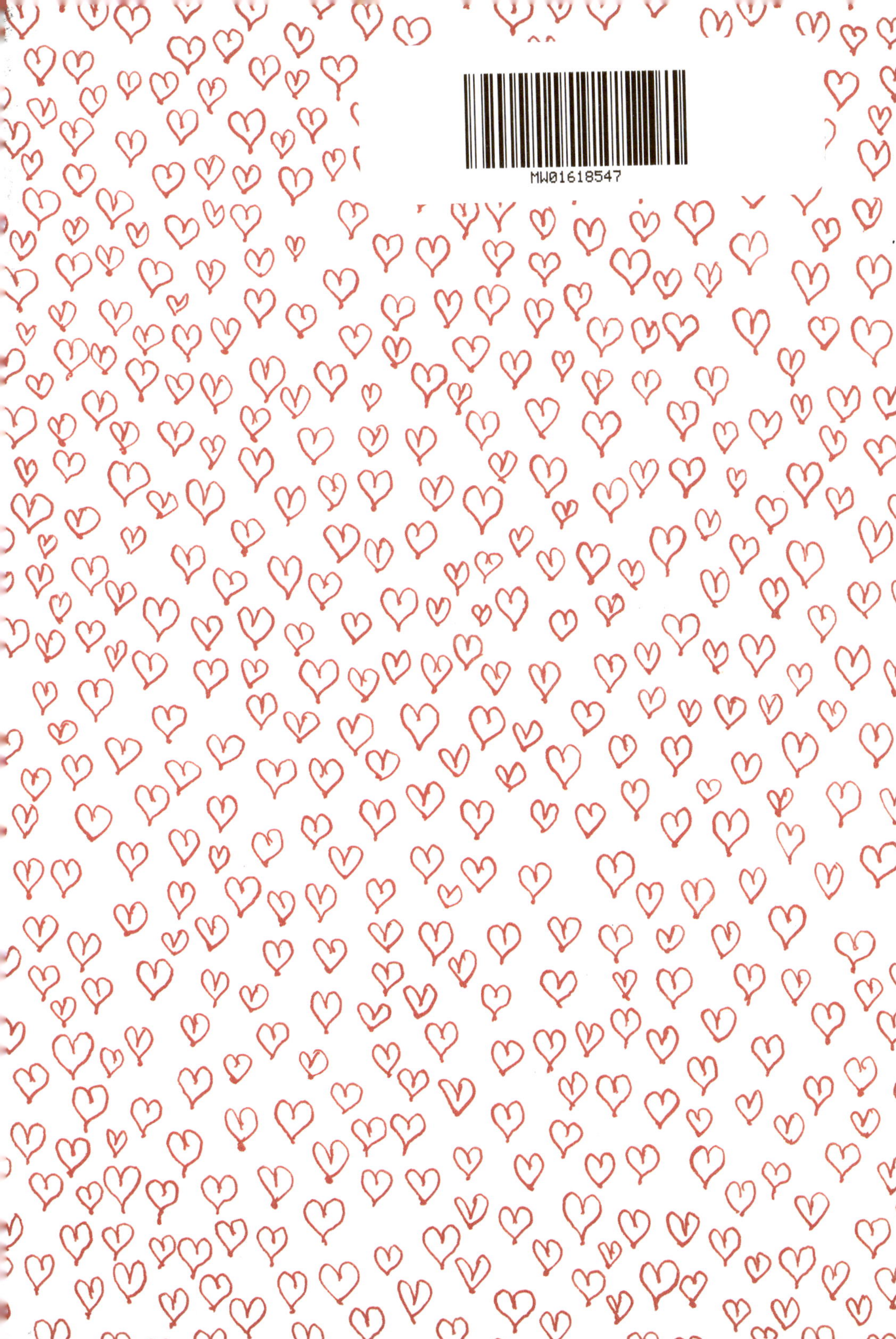

LOVERS

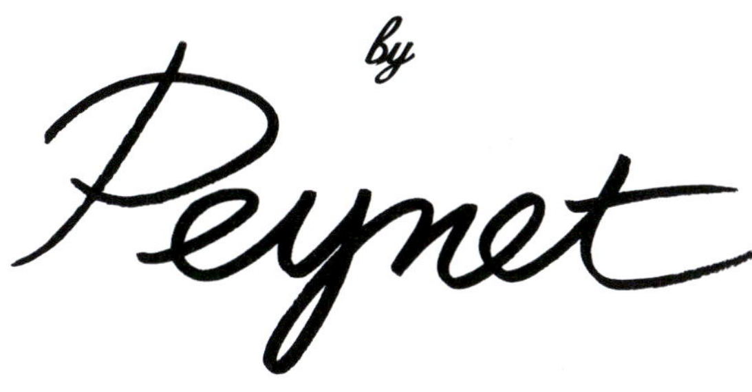

“I sat on a bench and sketched the bandstand before me; I drew a young violinist playing alone on the stage and a young girl listening, waiting.”

RAYMOND PEYNET, 1942

601 West 26th Street, 18th floor
New York, NY 10001
Tel.: 212 989-6810 Fax: 212 647-0005
www.assouline.com

ISBN : 978 2 75940 526 8
Translated from the French by Denise Raab Jacobs
Color separation by Planète Couleurs (France)
Printed by Grafiche Milani (Italy)

Cover: *Le Bouquet d'hirondelles* (A Bouquet of Swallows). Aquarelle drawing, 1960.
Flap: Heart design from the 1960s.

LOVERS

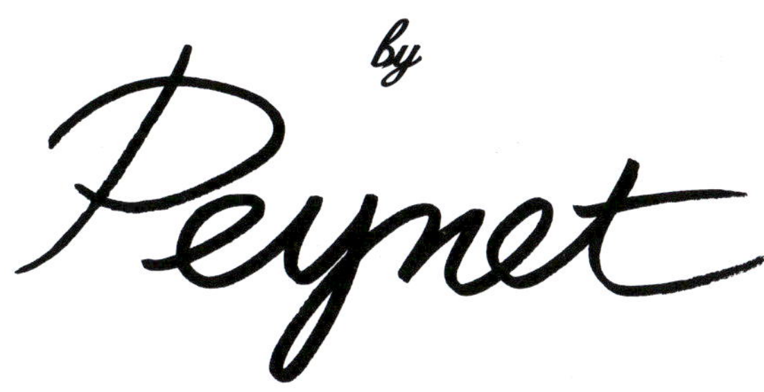

FROM THE AMUSED PERSPECTIVE
OF PLANTU

ASSOULINE

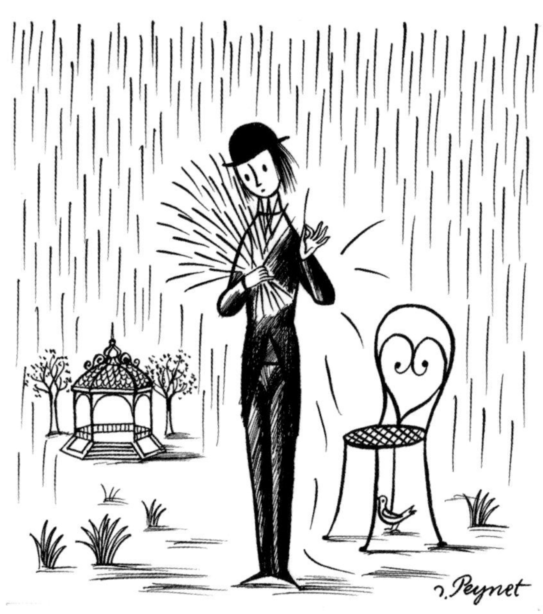

"Will come, won't come, will come, won't come..."
Pen and ink drawing.

Peynet: More Than Meets the Eye

Look at a Raymond Peynet illustration and the first thing you notice is the eyes, then the nose, the mouth, and the hat —his signature features. One line defines the ridge of the nose, beginning at the tip and reaching beyond the eyebrows— a style that was typical of his time (think of Antoine de Saint-Exupéry's *Little Prince*). The eyes evoke innocence, and the mouth—a little dot or a small line—is never vulgar.

Furthermore, the delicacy of the line draws you into a world of fantasy, an ambience of pleasure and love. In Peynet's day, illustrators took their time and invited the viewer to do the same when contemplating a drawing. Peynet occasionally used pastels and gouache (materials reminiscent of childhood) to create a warm and peaceful atmosphere. Today, these color tones are seldom used: In the digital world of the Internet and Photoshop, hardly anyone remembers gouache.

This is a far cry from the years of *Charlie*, the French satirical magazine: You never see tongues or teeth, both considered vulgar in Peynet's time. Still, his drawings, such as the one pictured here, often include more than meets the eye. You are fooled by the supposed innocence of the setting. In this case, a young man is making a bouquet out of rain—the sketched lines used to depict rain. But will he be able to hold onto them? "I love you, I love you not. . . ." The lovers' bandstand is behind him, and a little bird takes shelter under a chair; all seems pleasant. Love and tenderness are in the air. Yet there is always an acerbic element present, something that is not quite right. Peynet cleverly skirts censorship with great dexterity, slipping many elements into his drawings, shielded by his use of a simple line and feigned modesty. In 1961, the satirical publication *Hara-Kiri* was censored for showing breasts. But when Peynet did so, all was forgiven because he presented them in a sweet and wholesome context: Ostensibly, he was interested in breasts because they are pretty and he thought they should be drawn. But there is no fornication depicted—he can only hint at something that is supposed to be love. He wants you to believe (though no one does) that the lovers might one day move on to the actual act. In the meantime, he will simply allude, in a saccharine manner, to the act of penetration, which you will never see. This is why his drawings appeal to a Japanese readership in particular, for nothing is ever blatant. The viewer is never humiliated or assaulted by his images: Women are demure, their eyes downcast; a bird rests discreetly on an opulent bosom; naked breasts are just part of the scenery. If a woman's face is completely shaded by her cloche hat, the viewer's eye is immediately drawn to her legs and the sway of her hips. In the end, what matters is what the reader will imagine, and Peynet will always claim to be surprised!

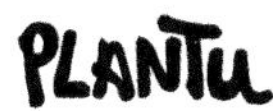

I love you so,
You love you so, we sow our love.

Maurice Chapelan

Lovers, Love

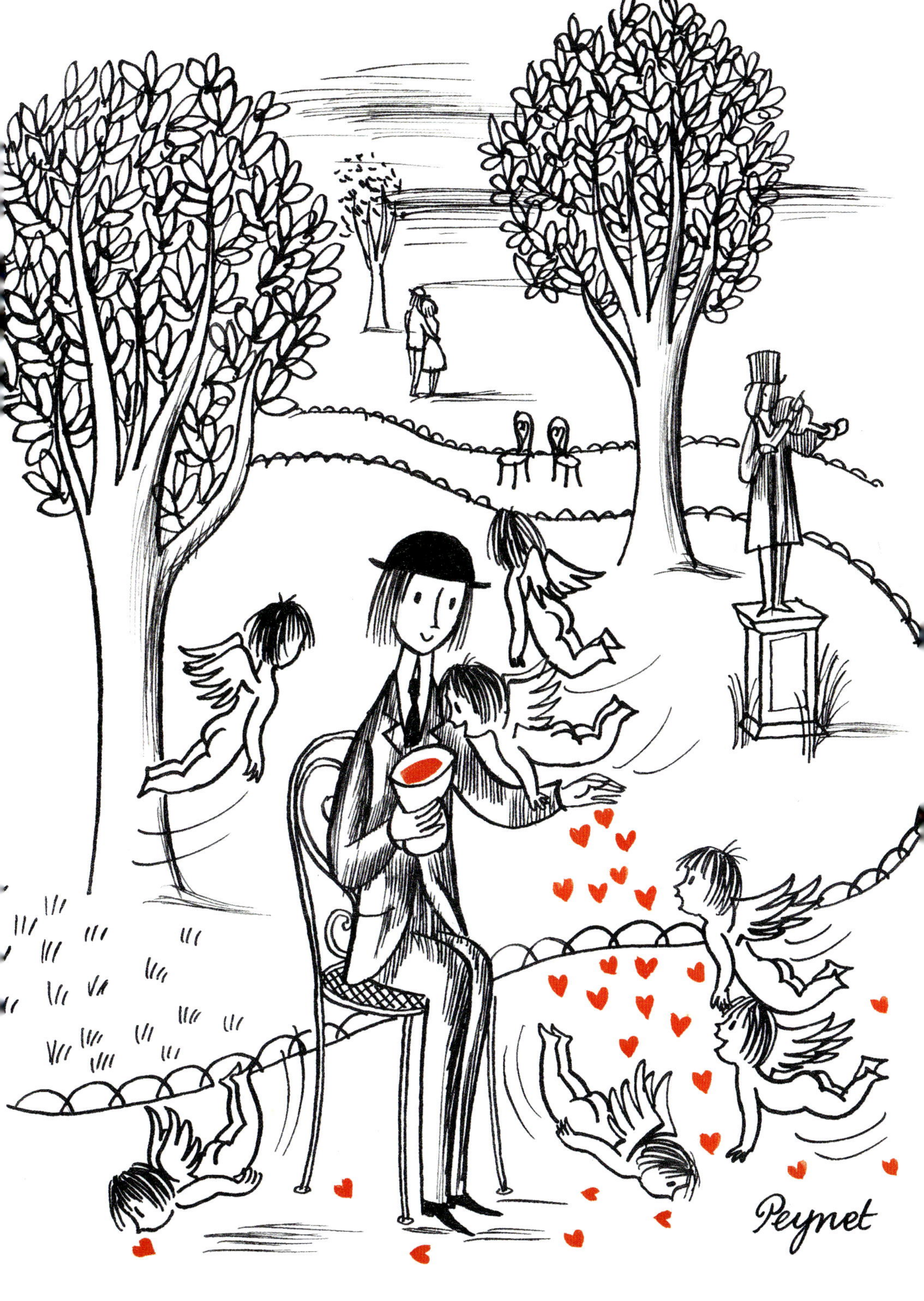
Peynet

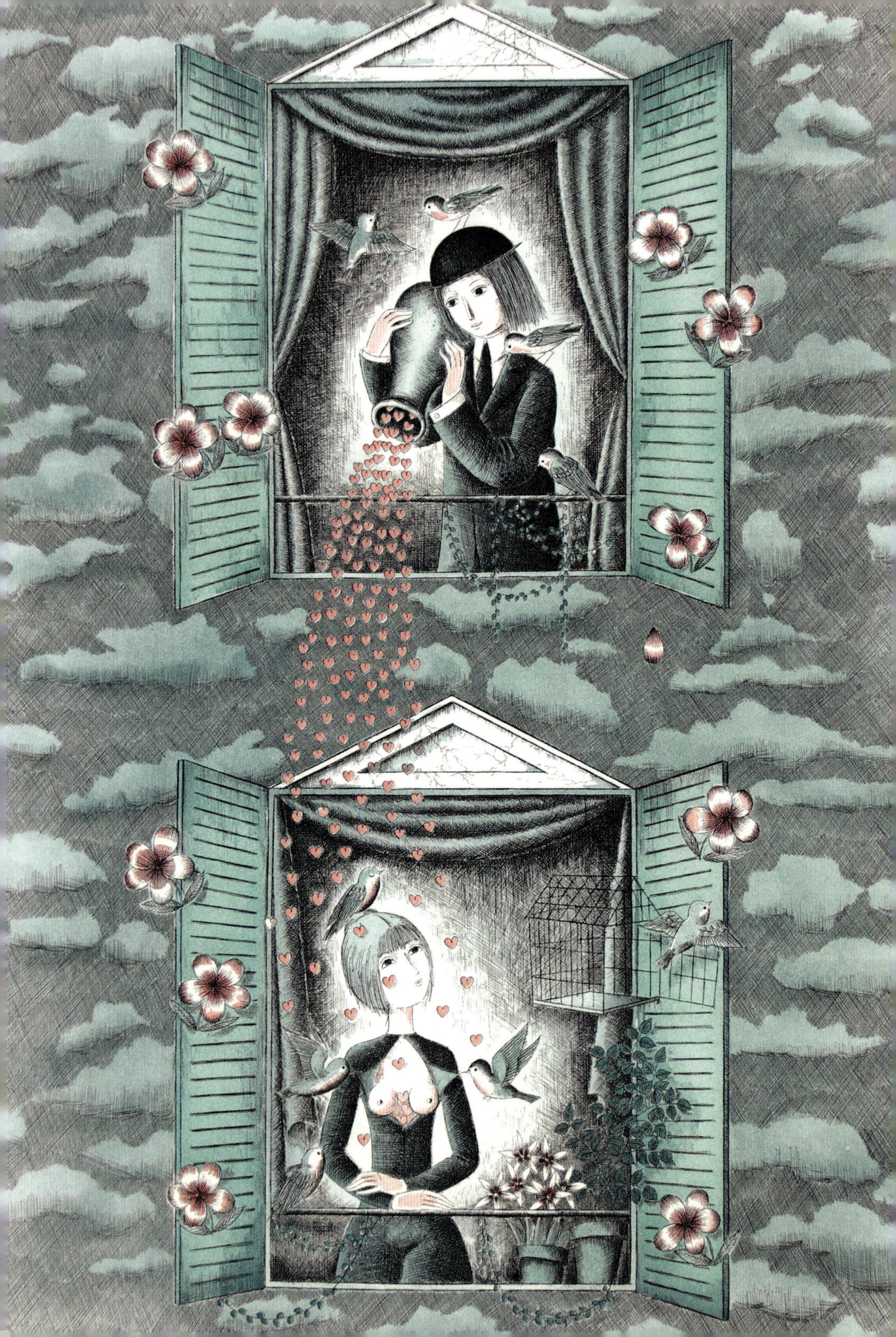

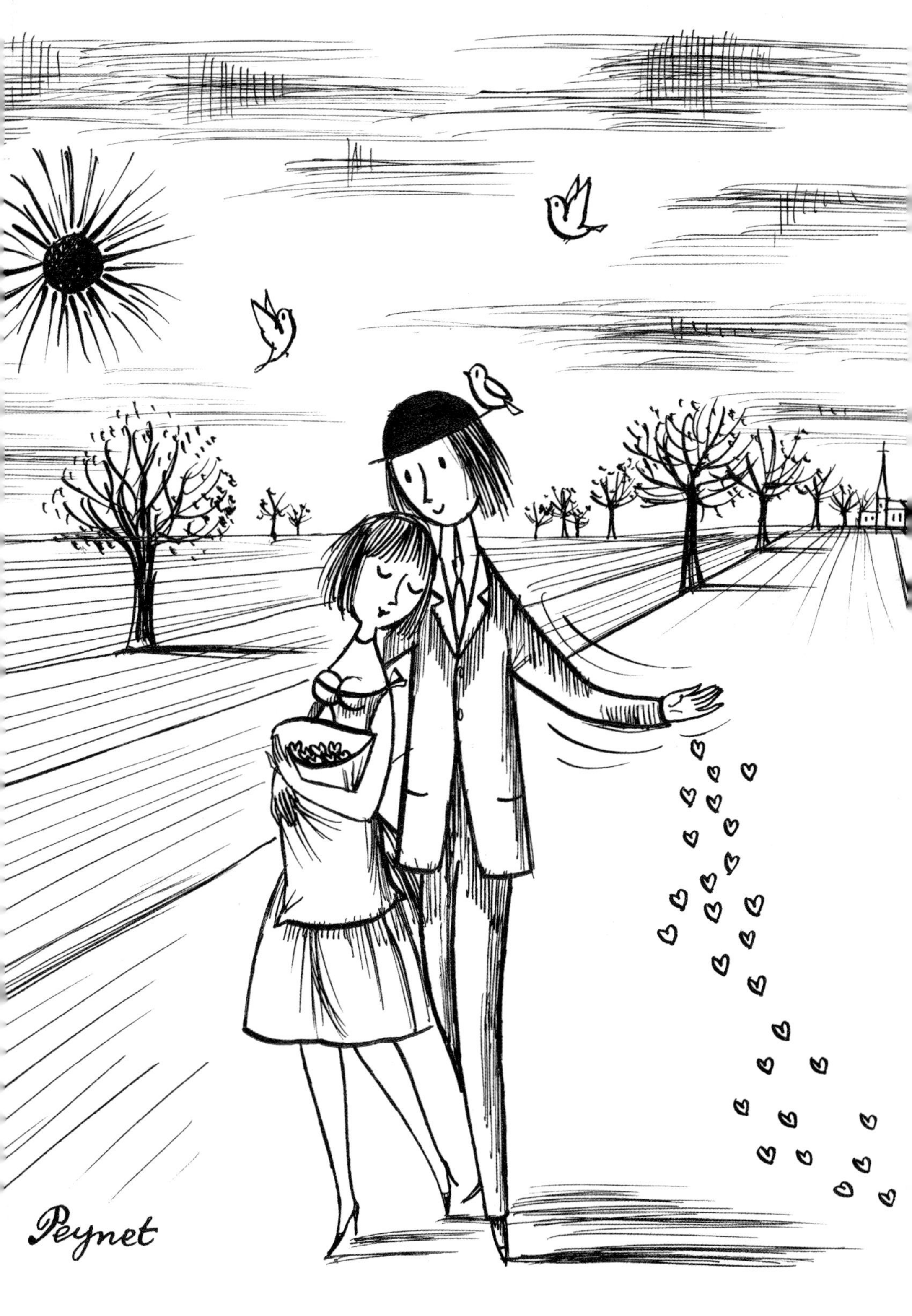
Peynet

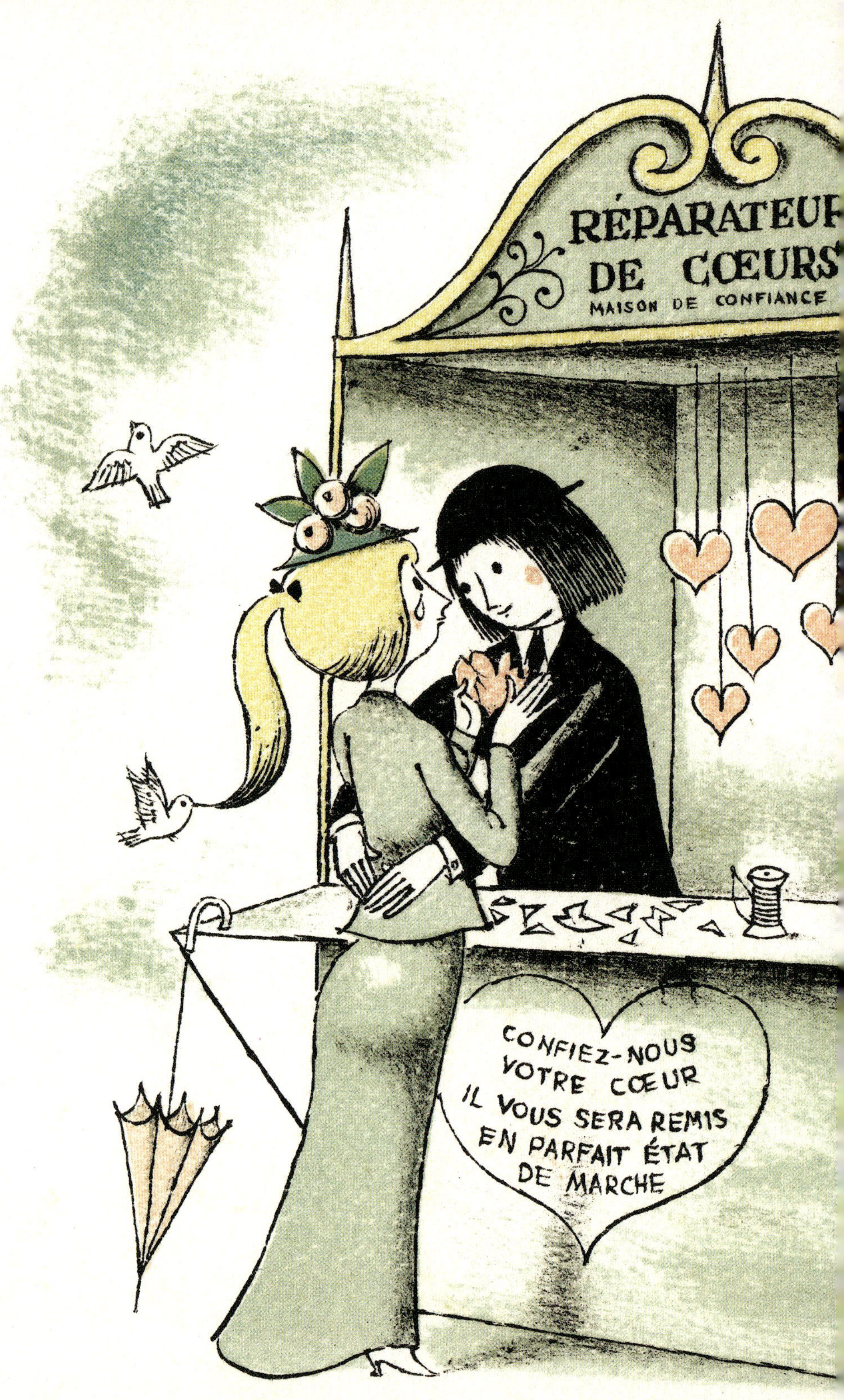
RÉPARATEUR
DE CŒURS
MAISON DE CONFIANCE
CONFIEZ-NOUS
VOTRE CŒUR
IL VOUS SERA REMIS
EN PARFAIT ÉTAT
DE MARCHE

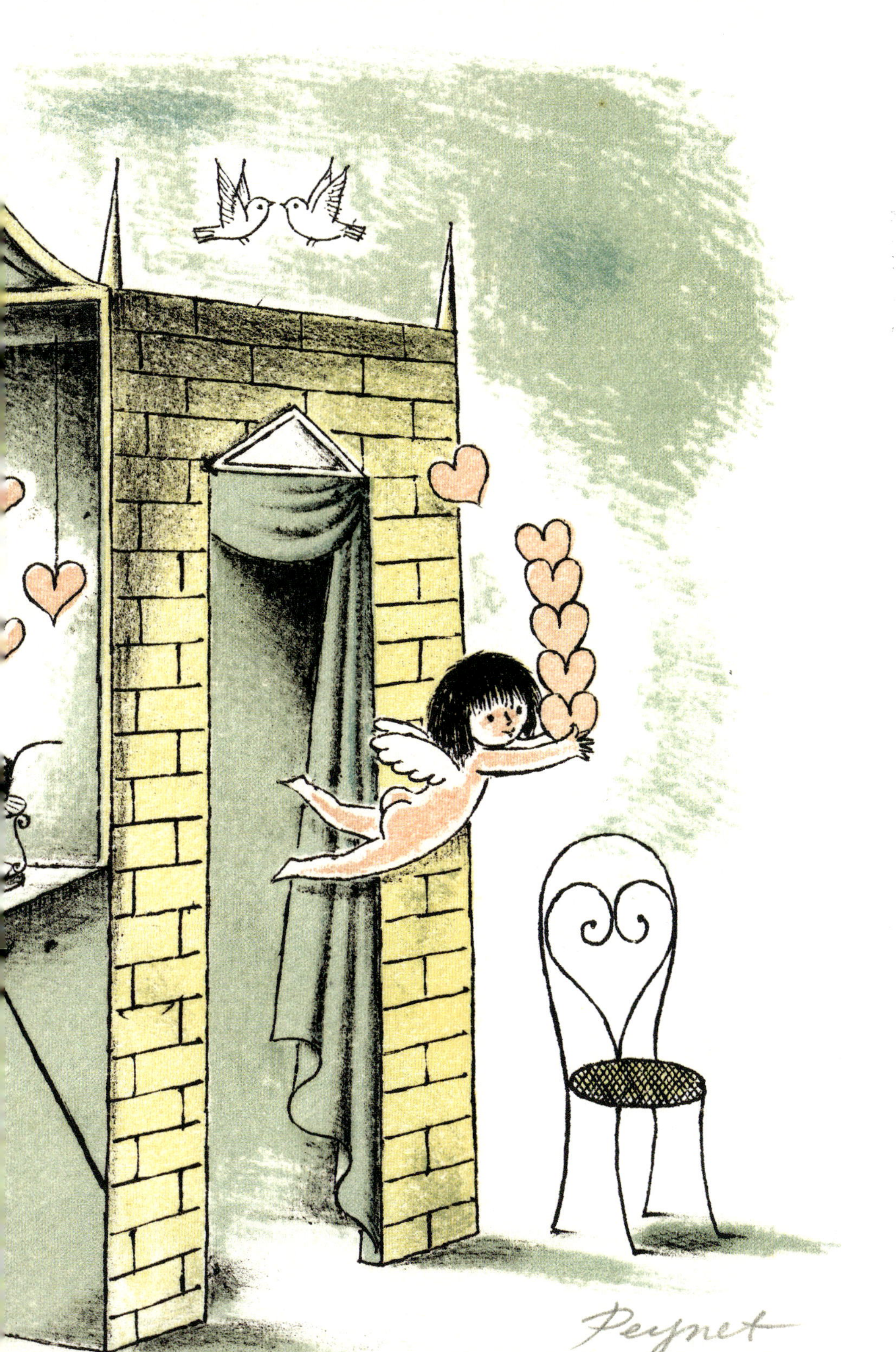
Peynet

It is only with the heart that one can see rightly; what is essential is invisible to the eye.

Antoine de Saint-Exupery
The Little Prince

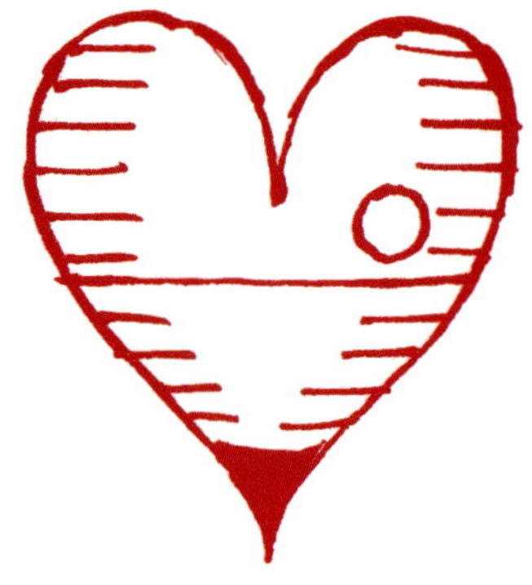

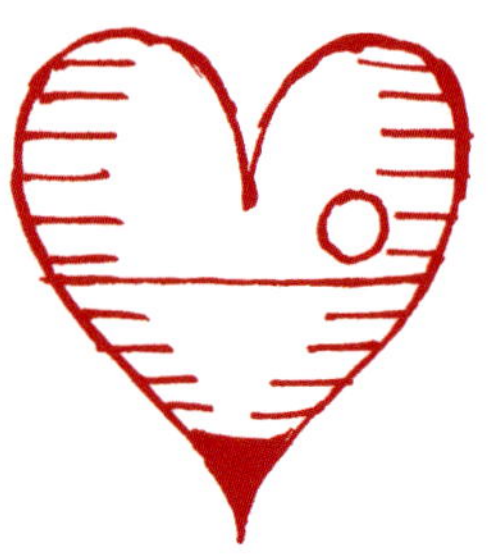

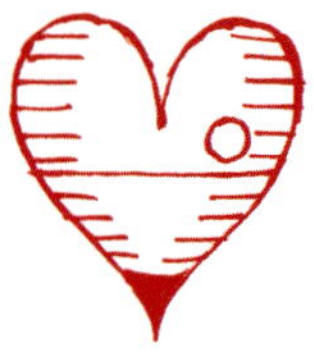

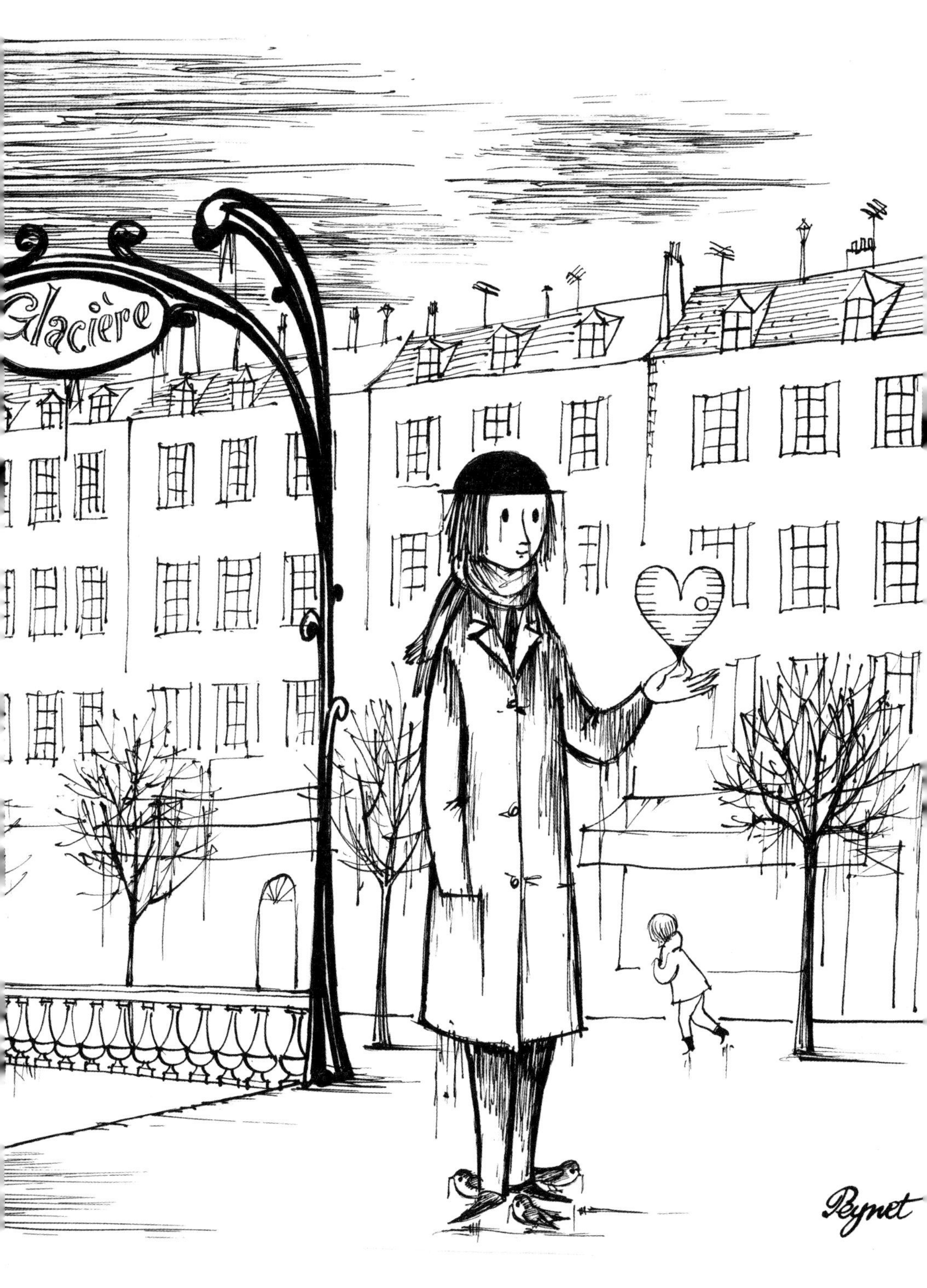
Glacière
Peynet

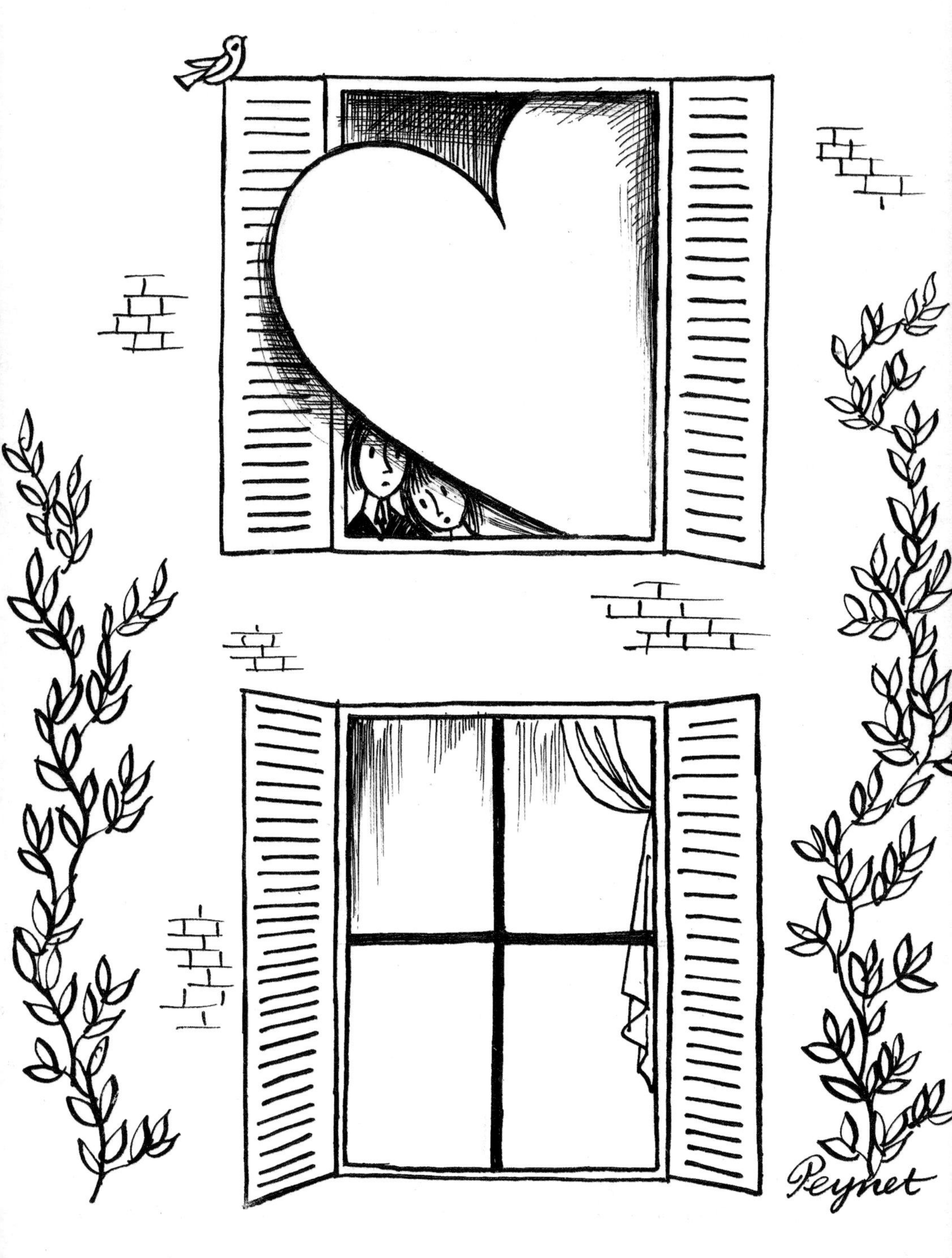
Peynet

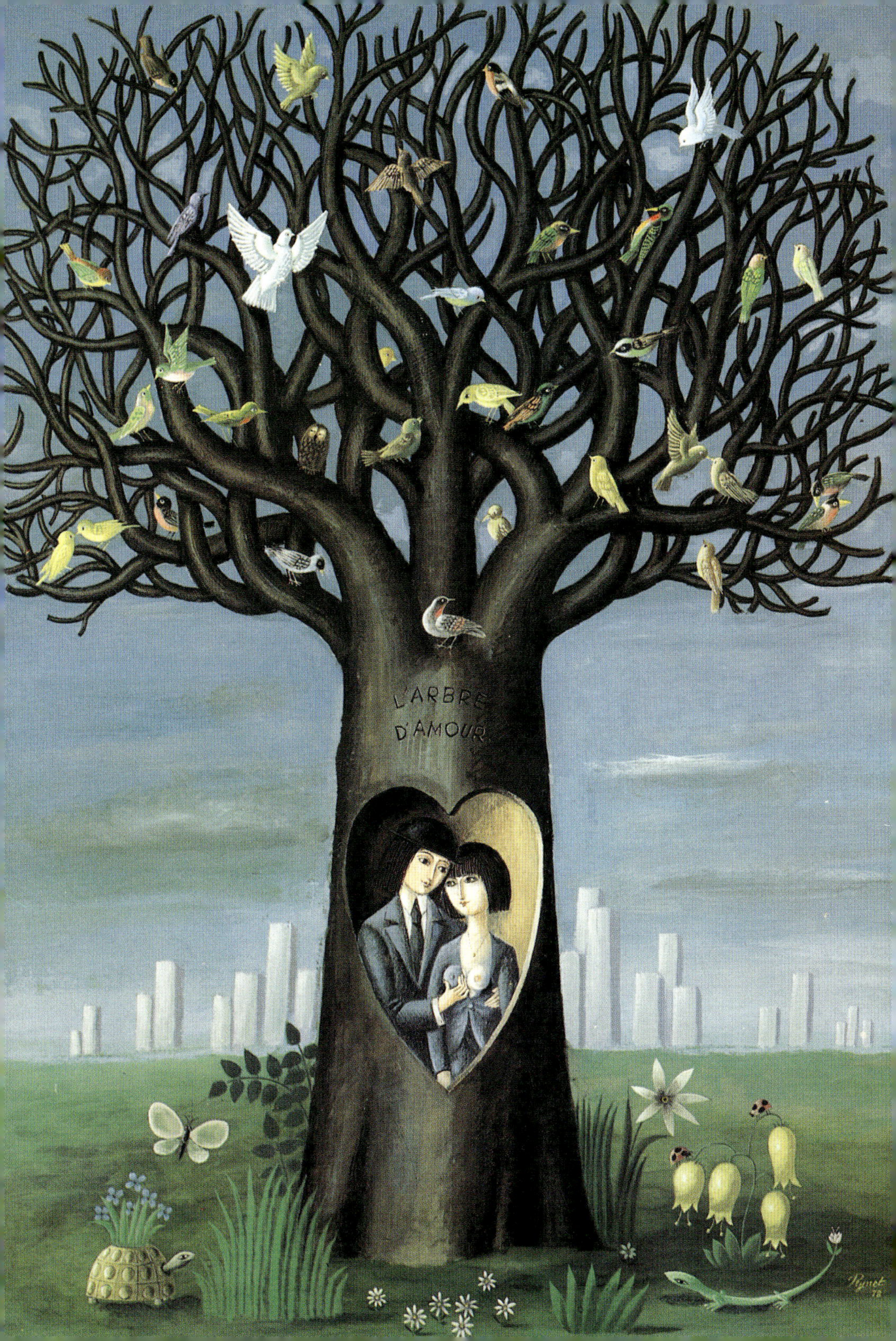
L'ARBRE
D'AMOUR

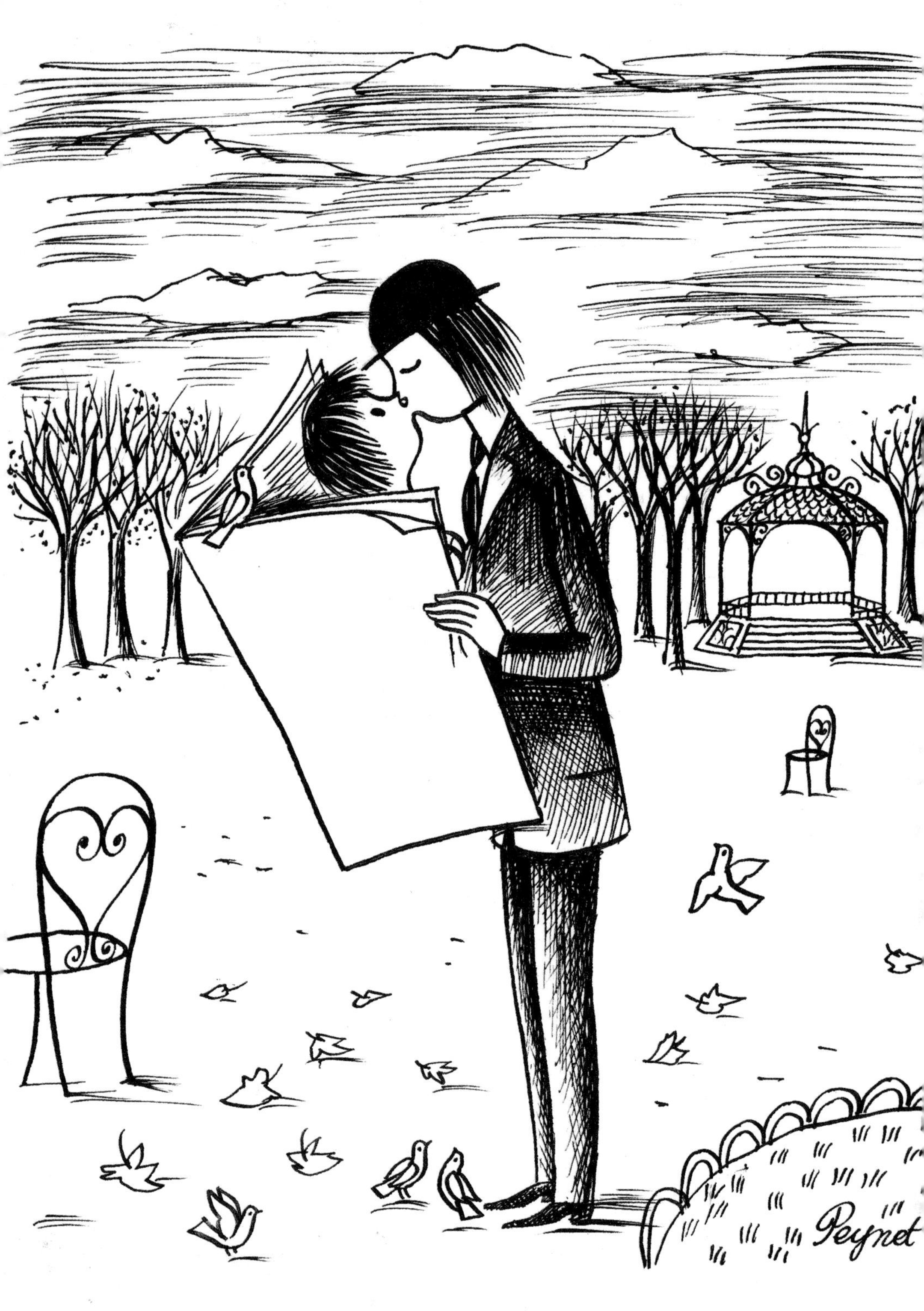
Peynet

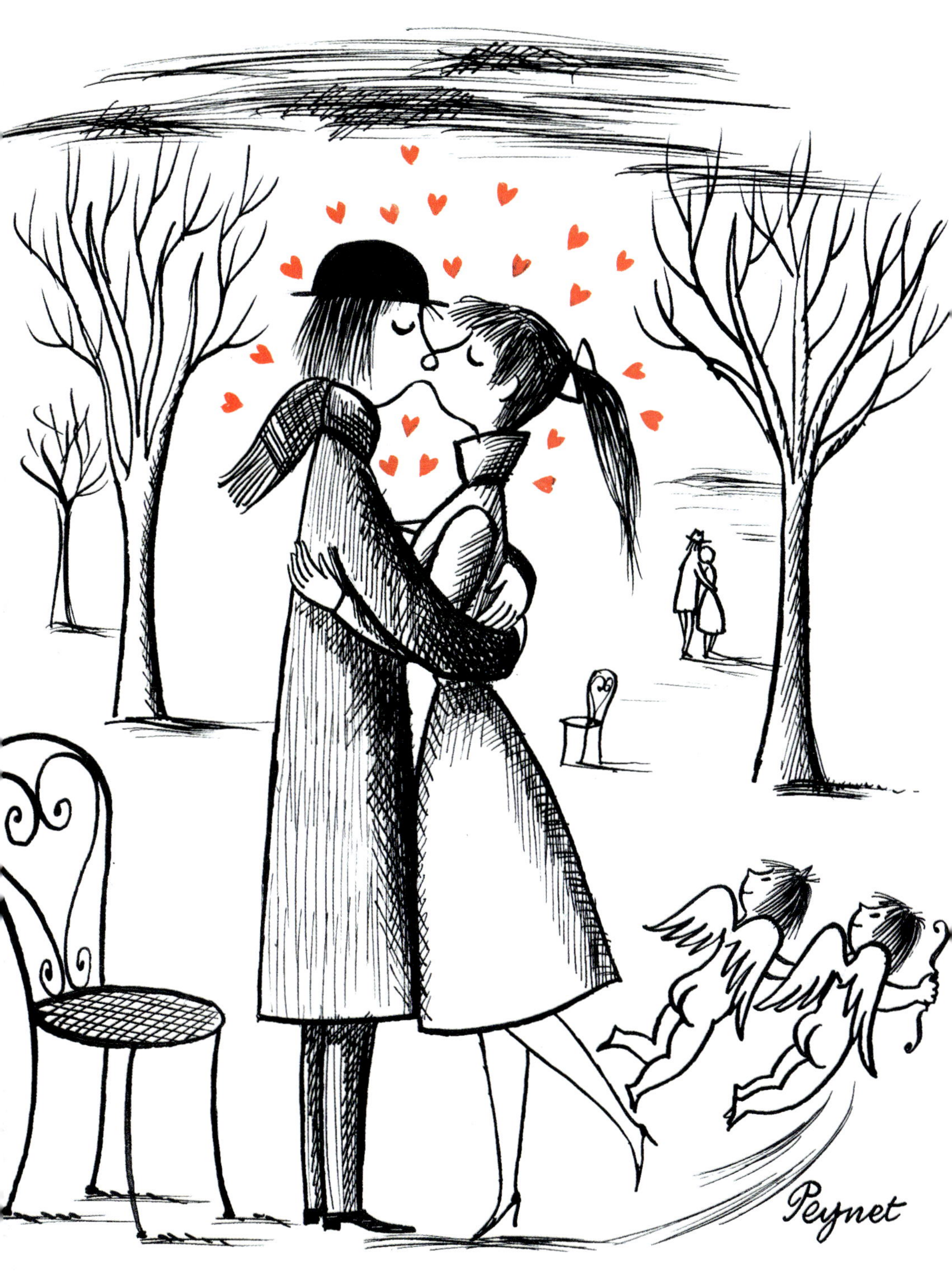
Peynet

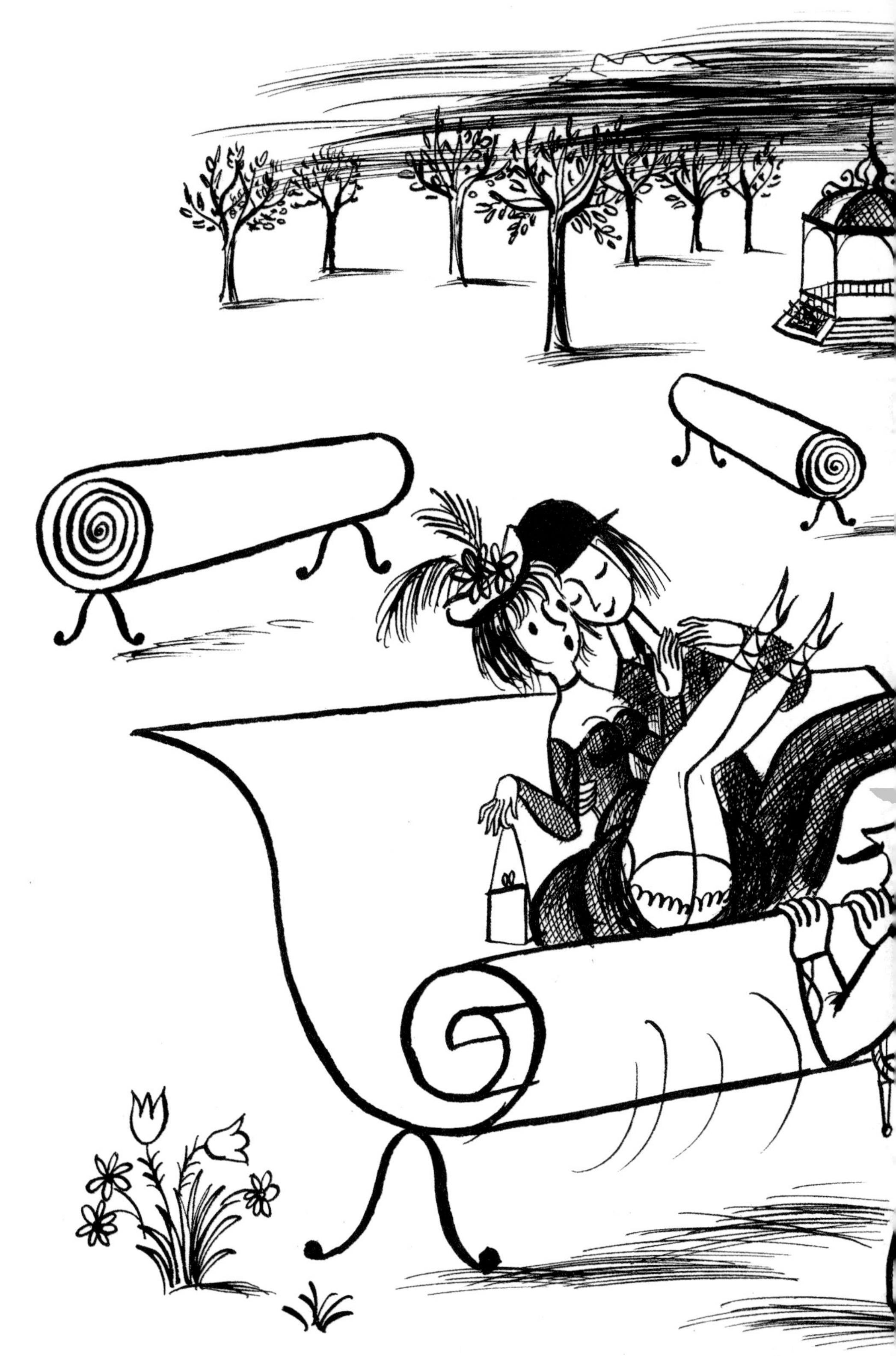

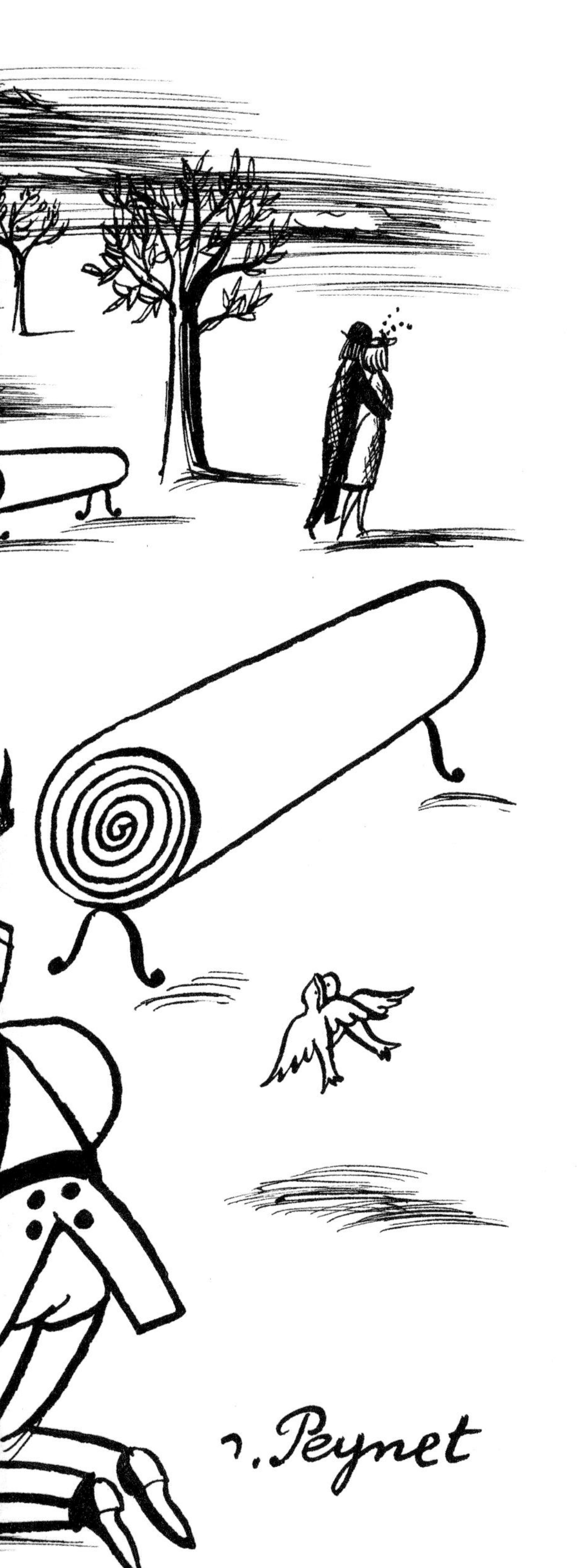
Peynet

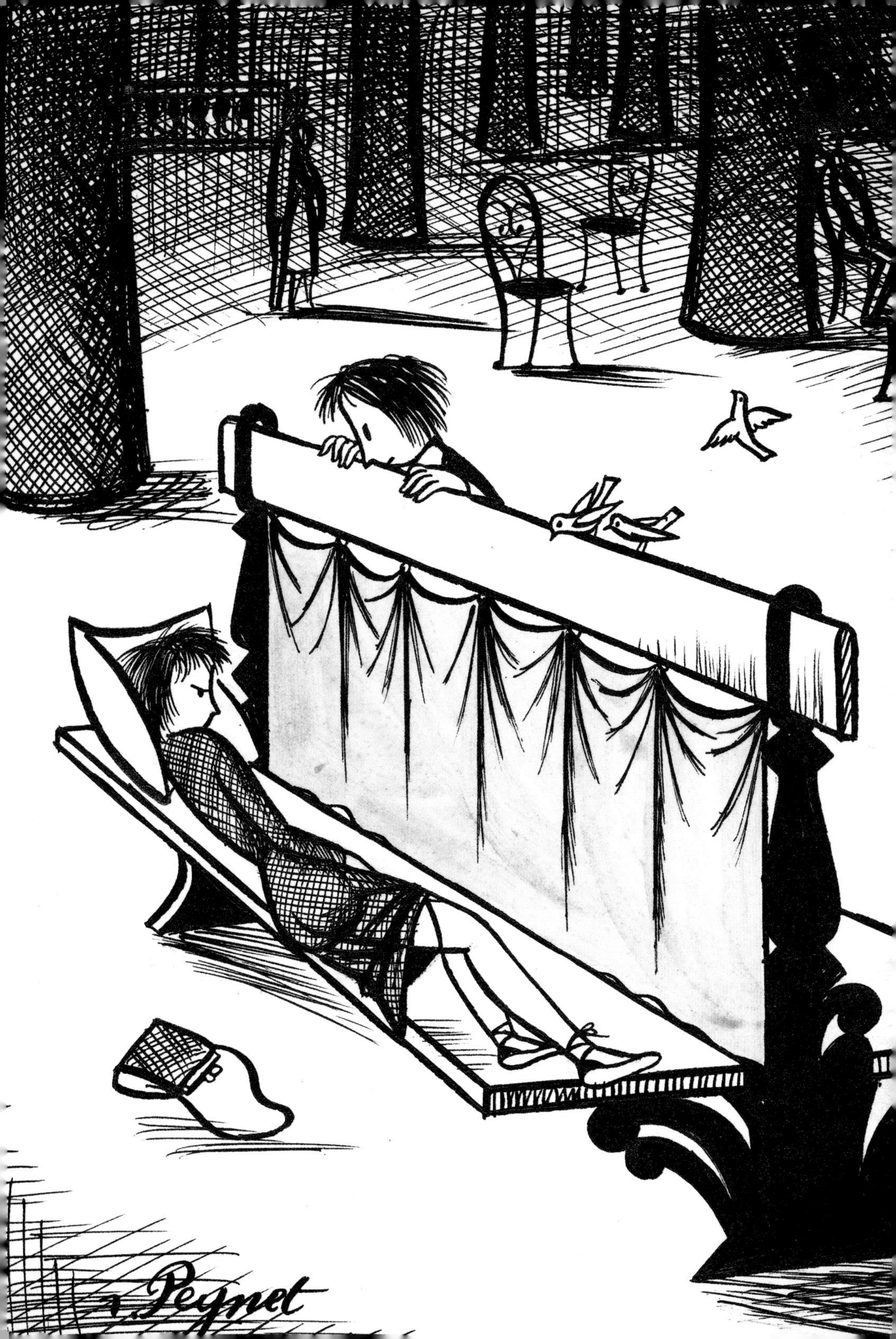
Peynet

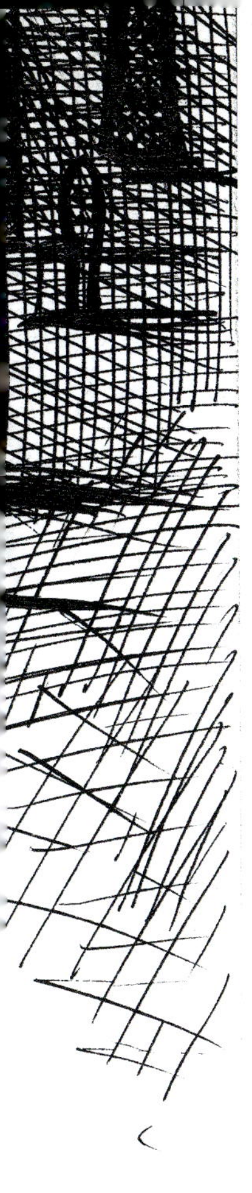

There is no love,
there are only
acts of love.

Pierre Reverdy

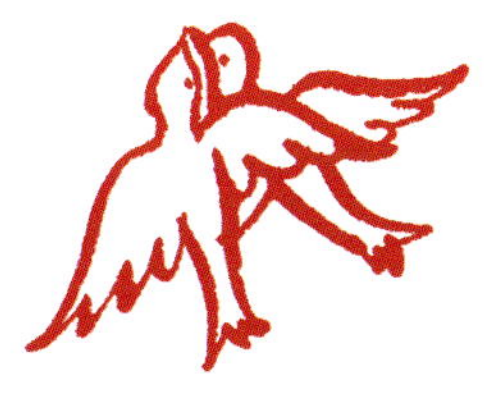

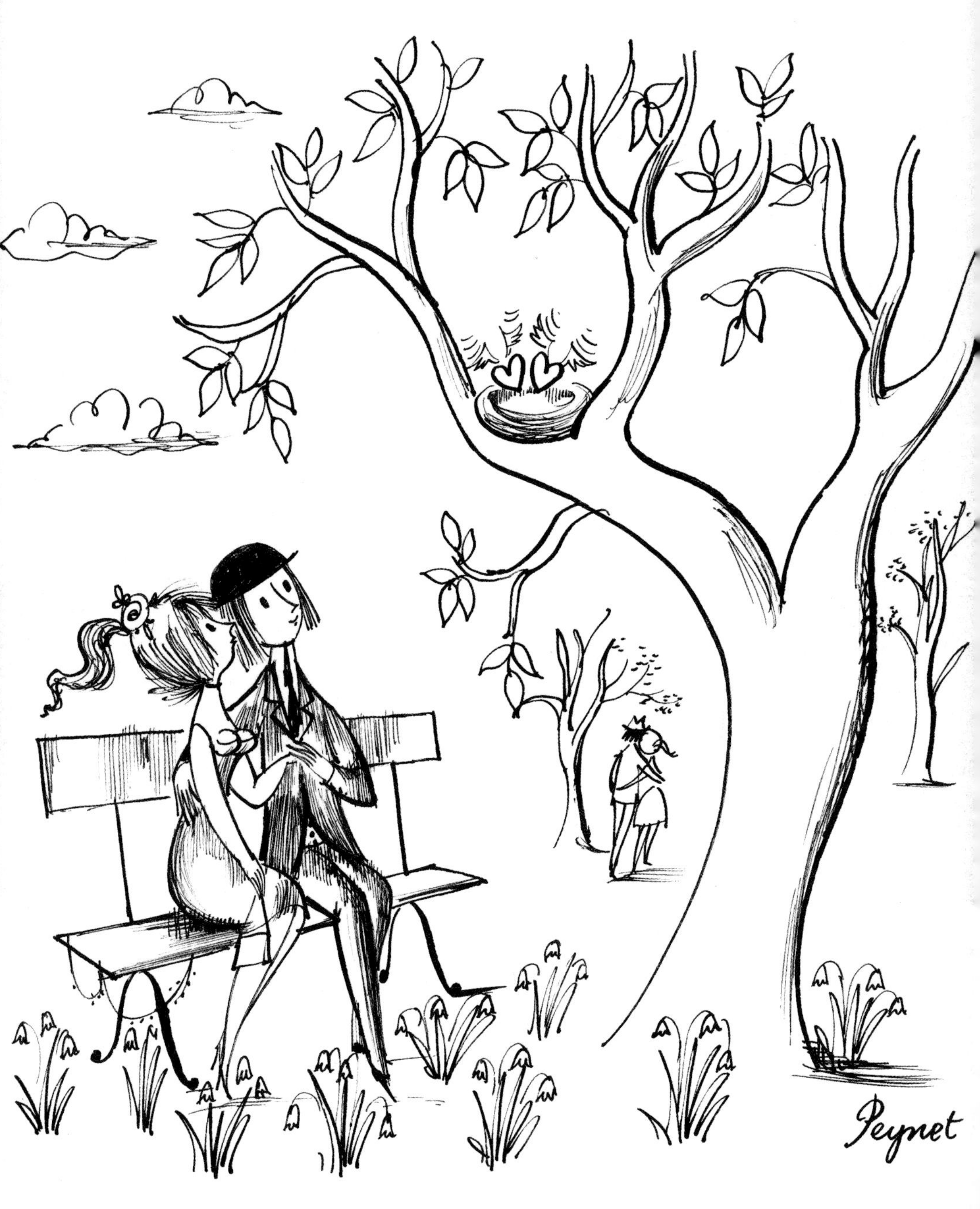
Peynet

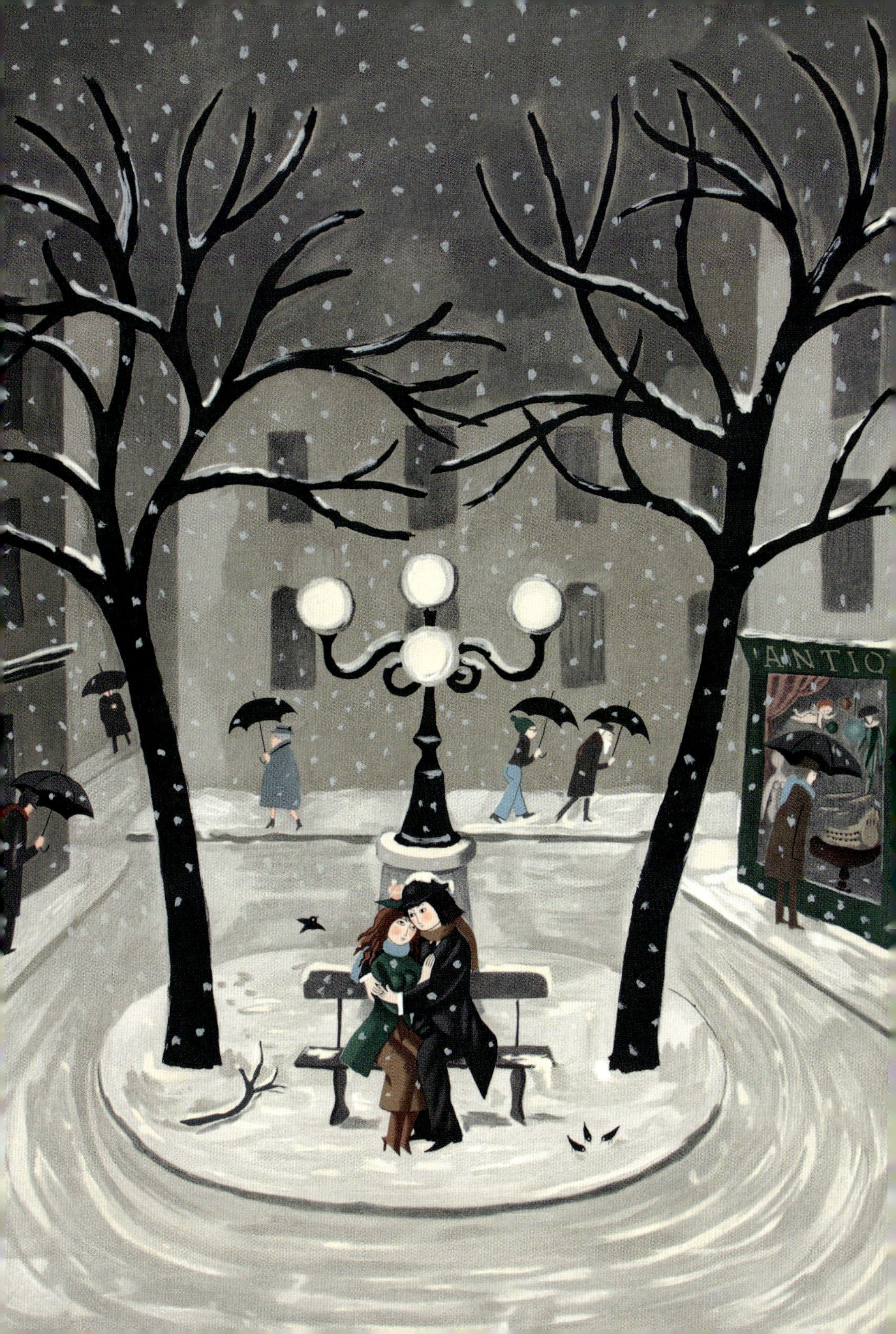
ANTIQ

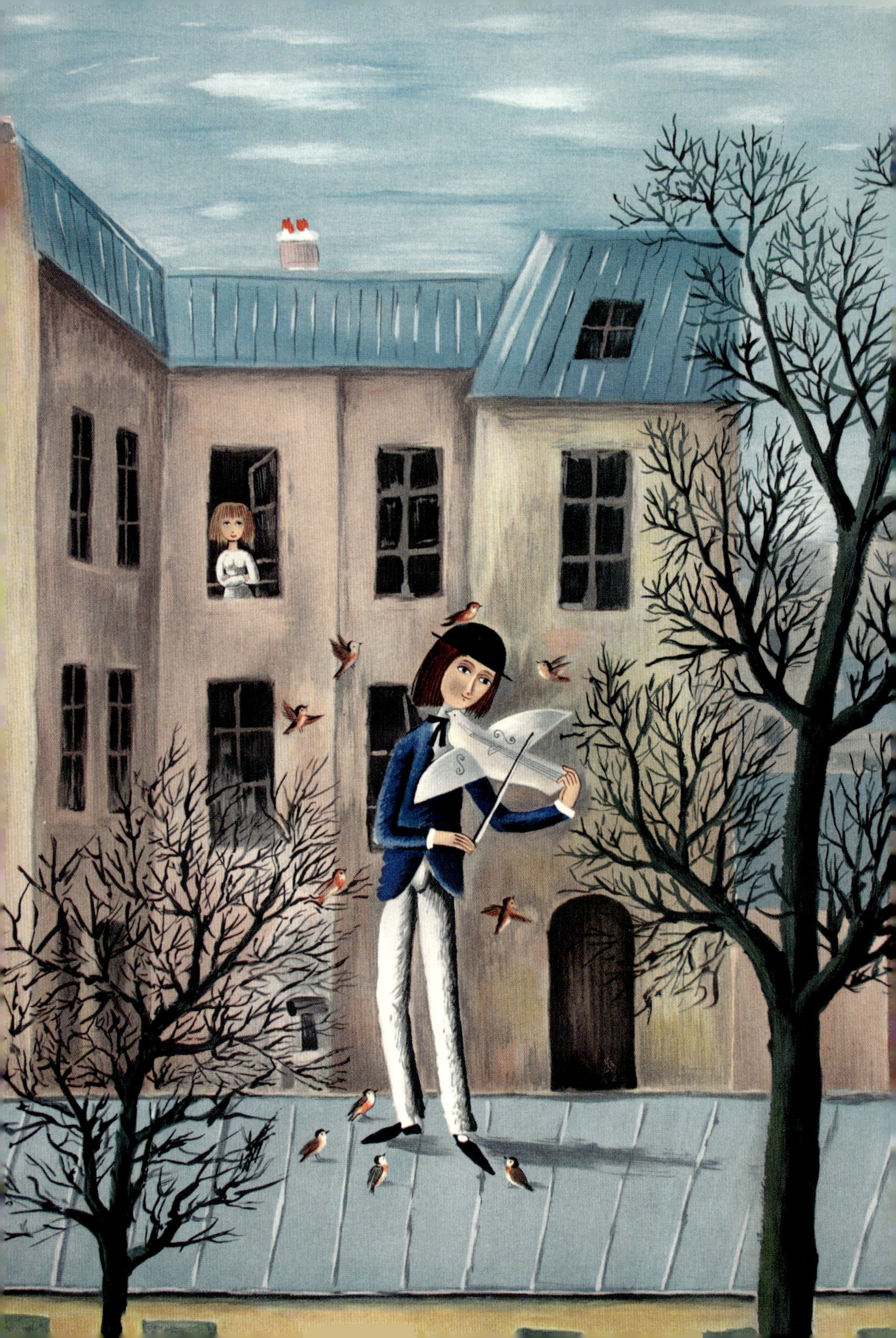

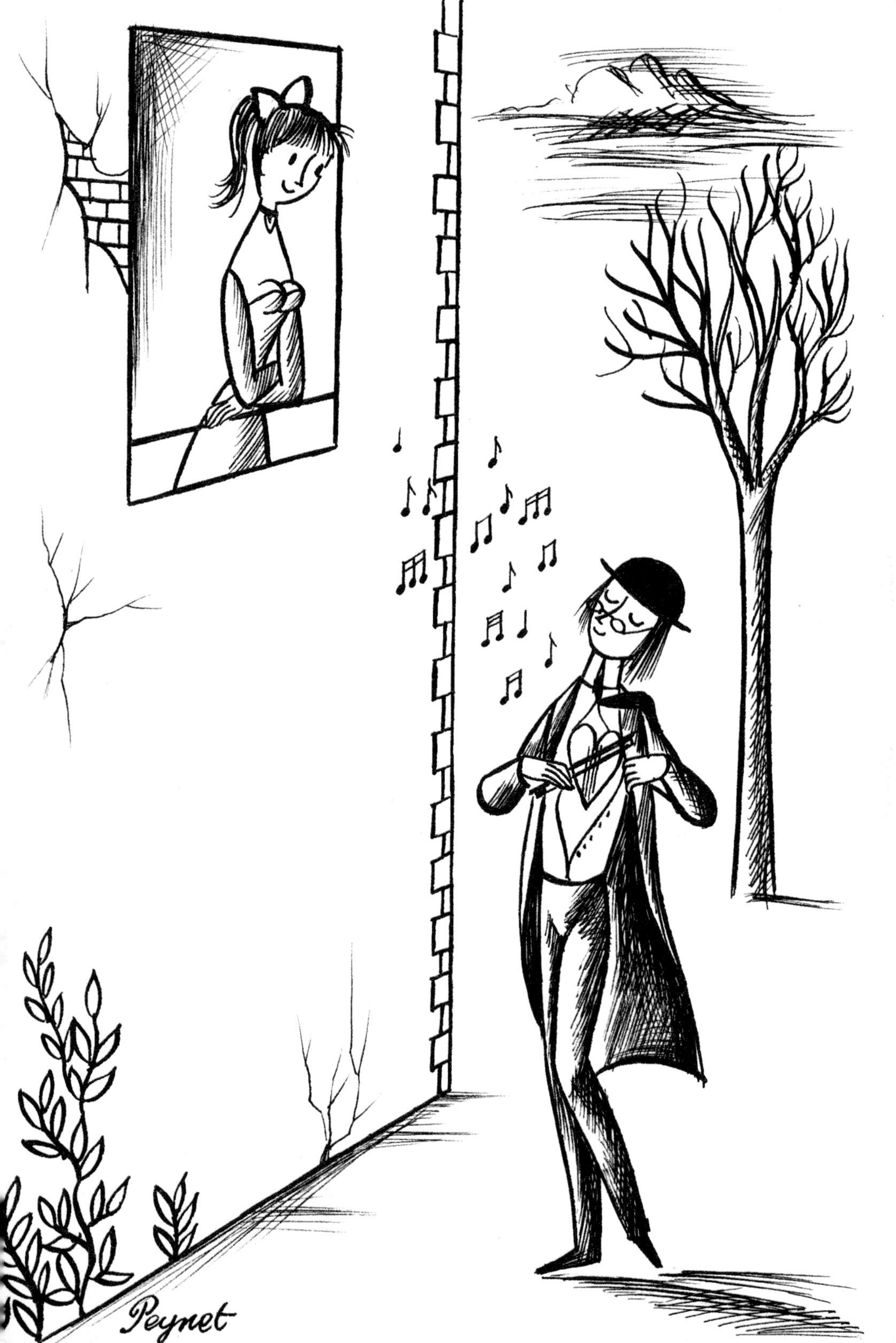
Peynet

If music be
the food of love,
play on.

WILLIAM SHAKESPEARE
Twelfth Night

Love is an art,
much like music.

PIERRE LOUŸS
Aphrodite

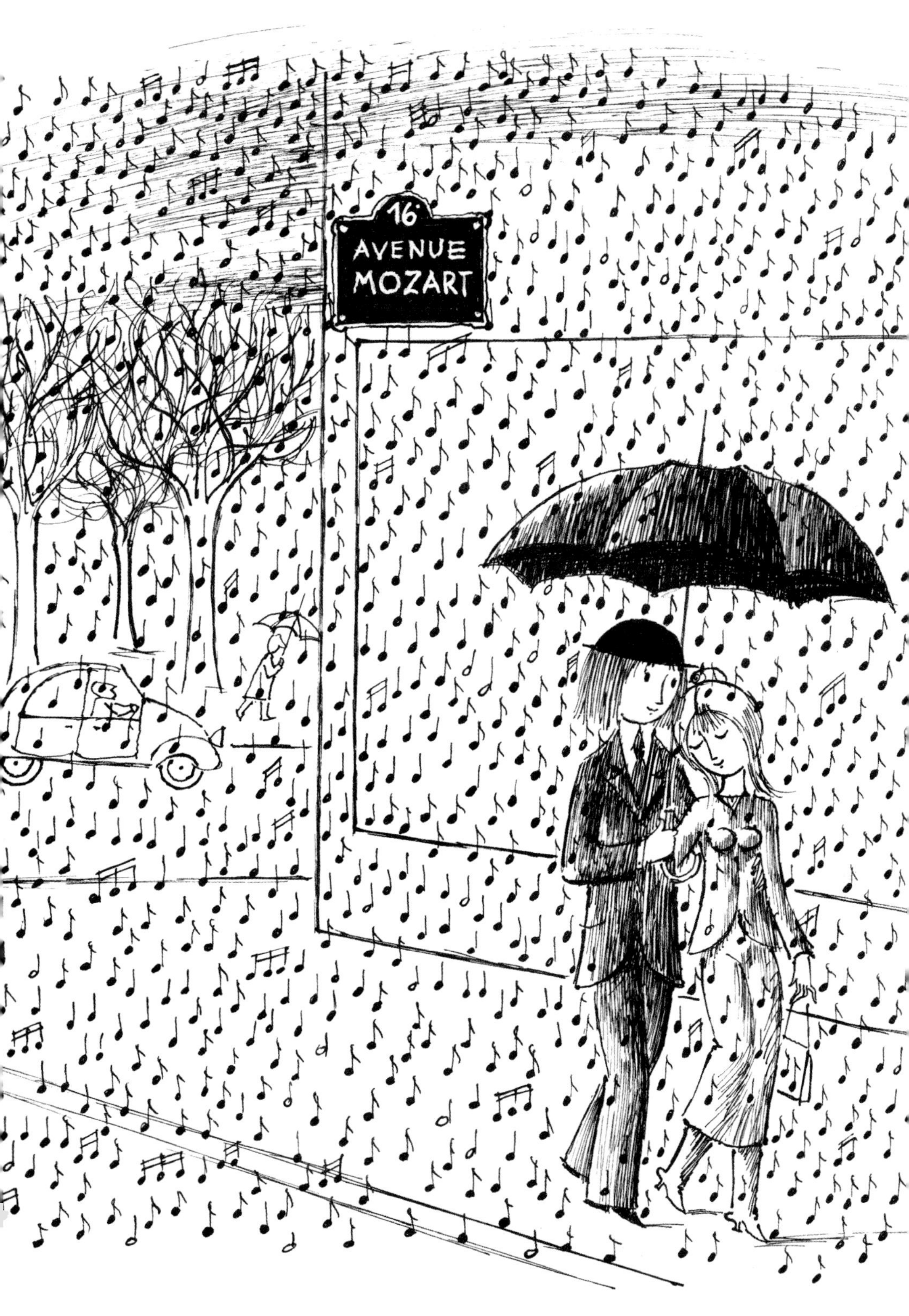
16e
AVENUE
MOZART

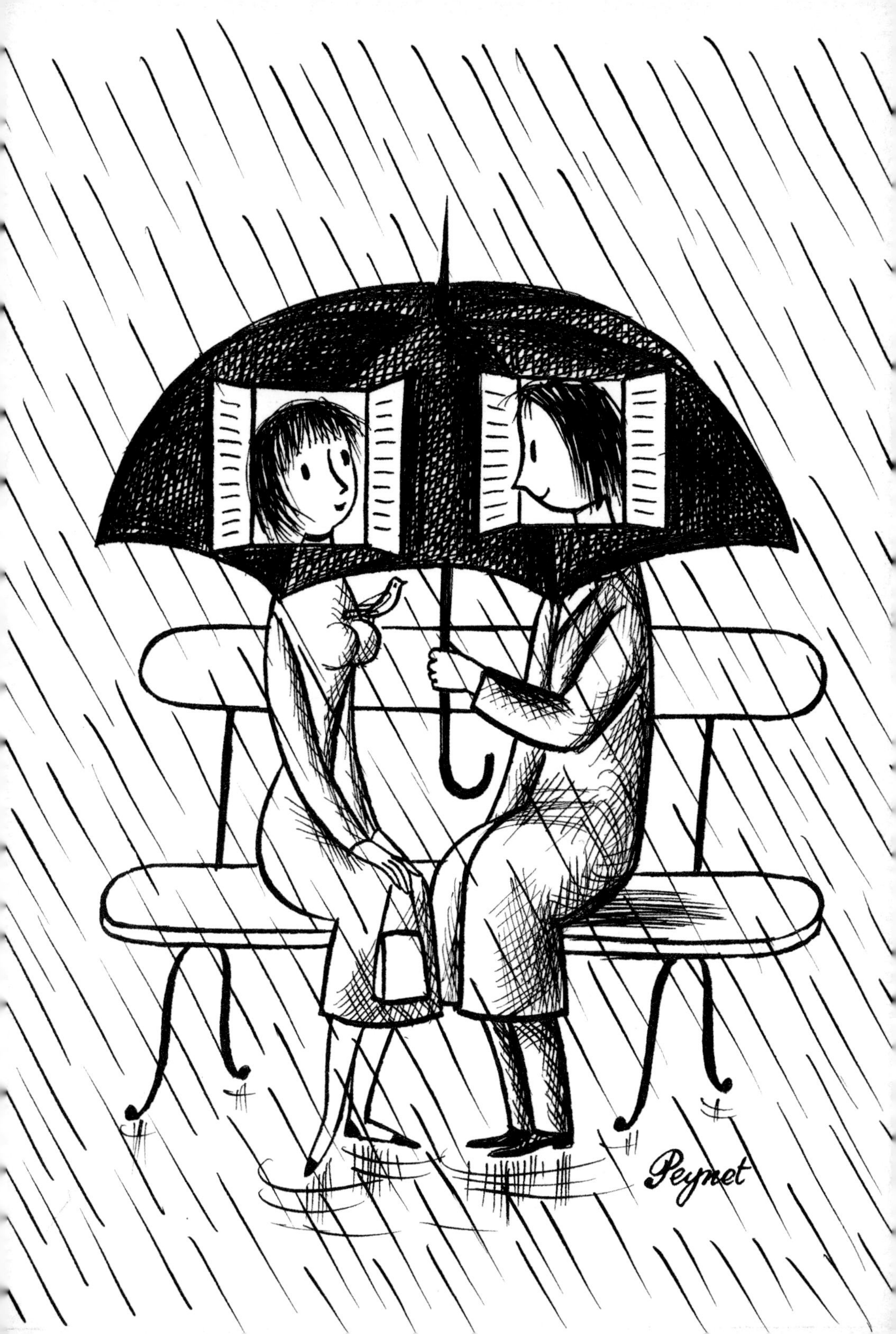
Peynet

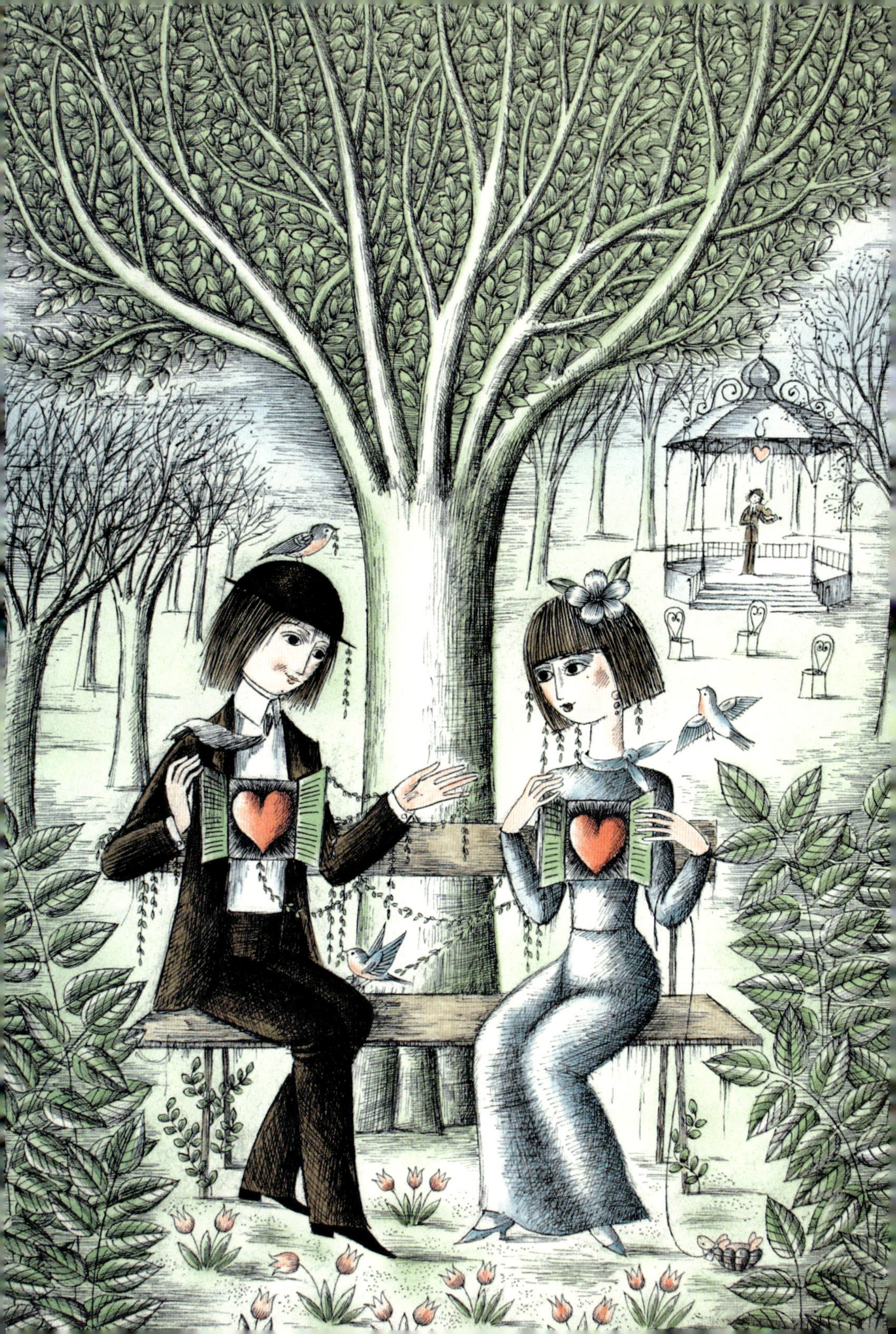

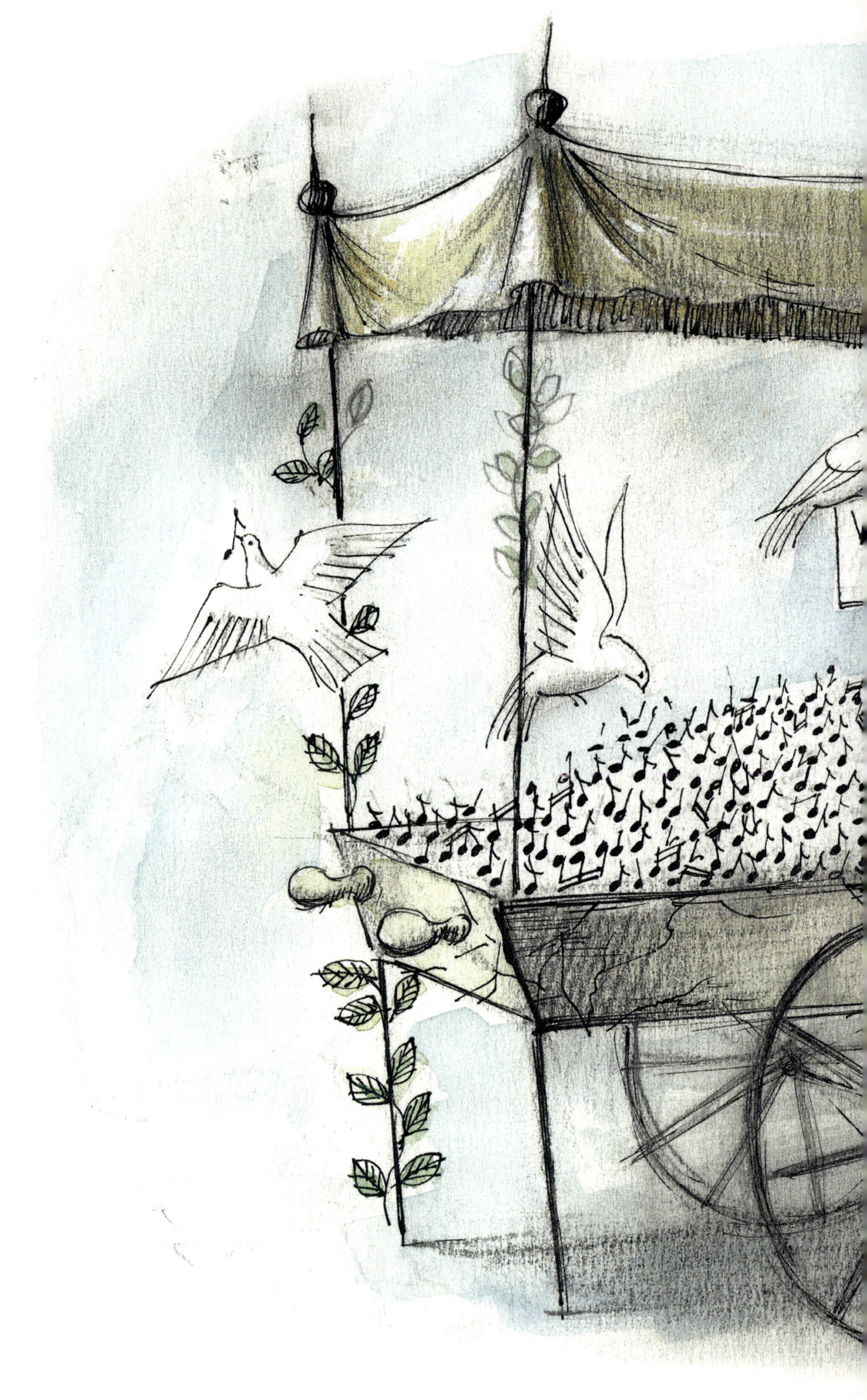

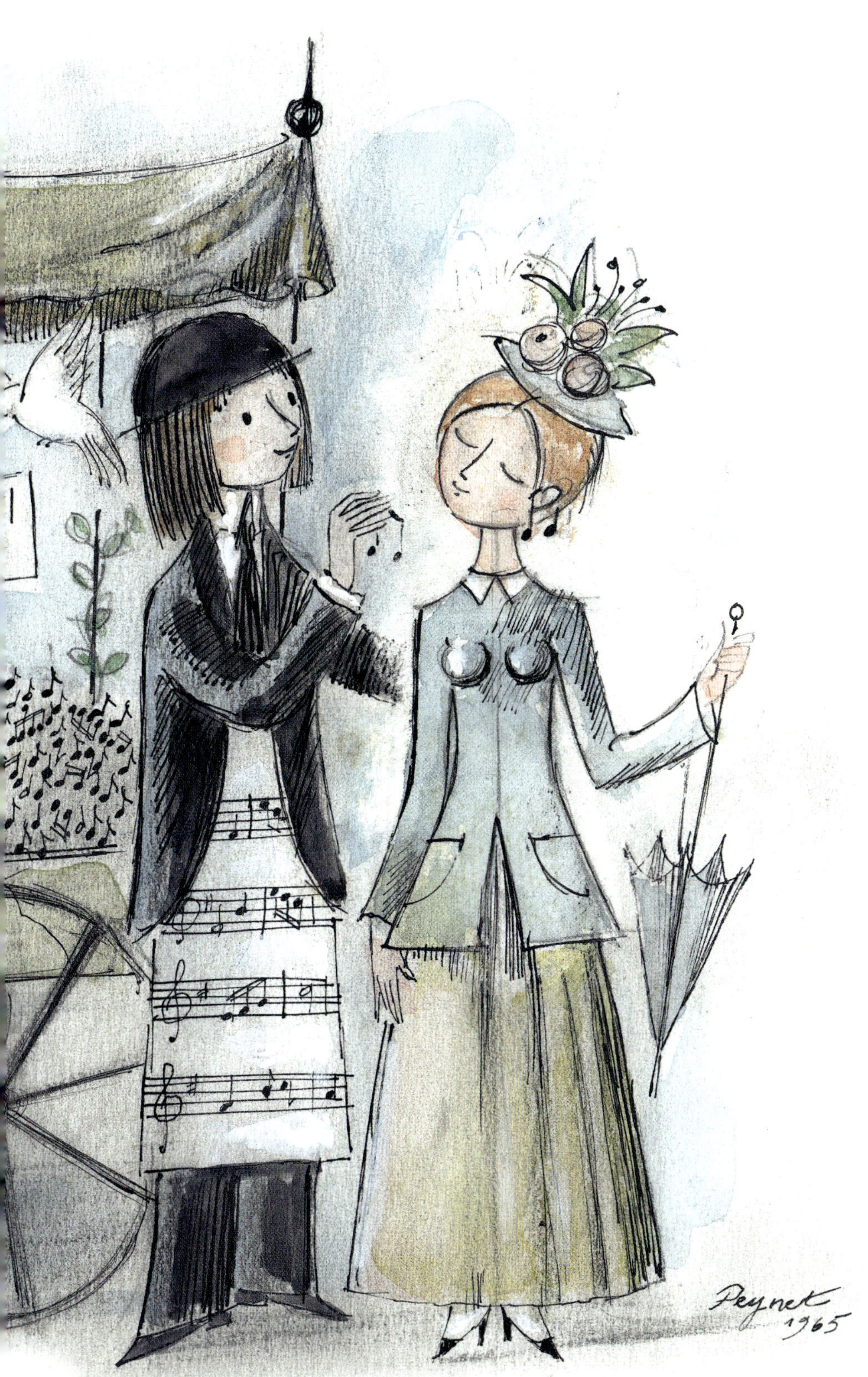
Peynet
1965

Paper
Lovers
Live on a cloud
They have the quaint look
Of lovers from past times
The paper lovers
Exchange gallantries
And promises of love
On hearts made of paper.

CHARLES AZNAVOUR
"Paper Lovers"

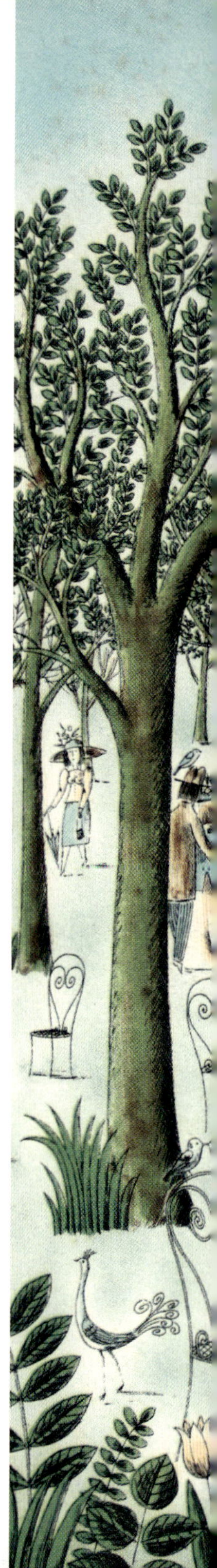

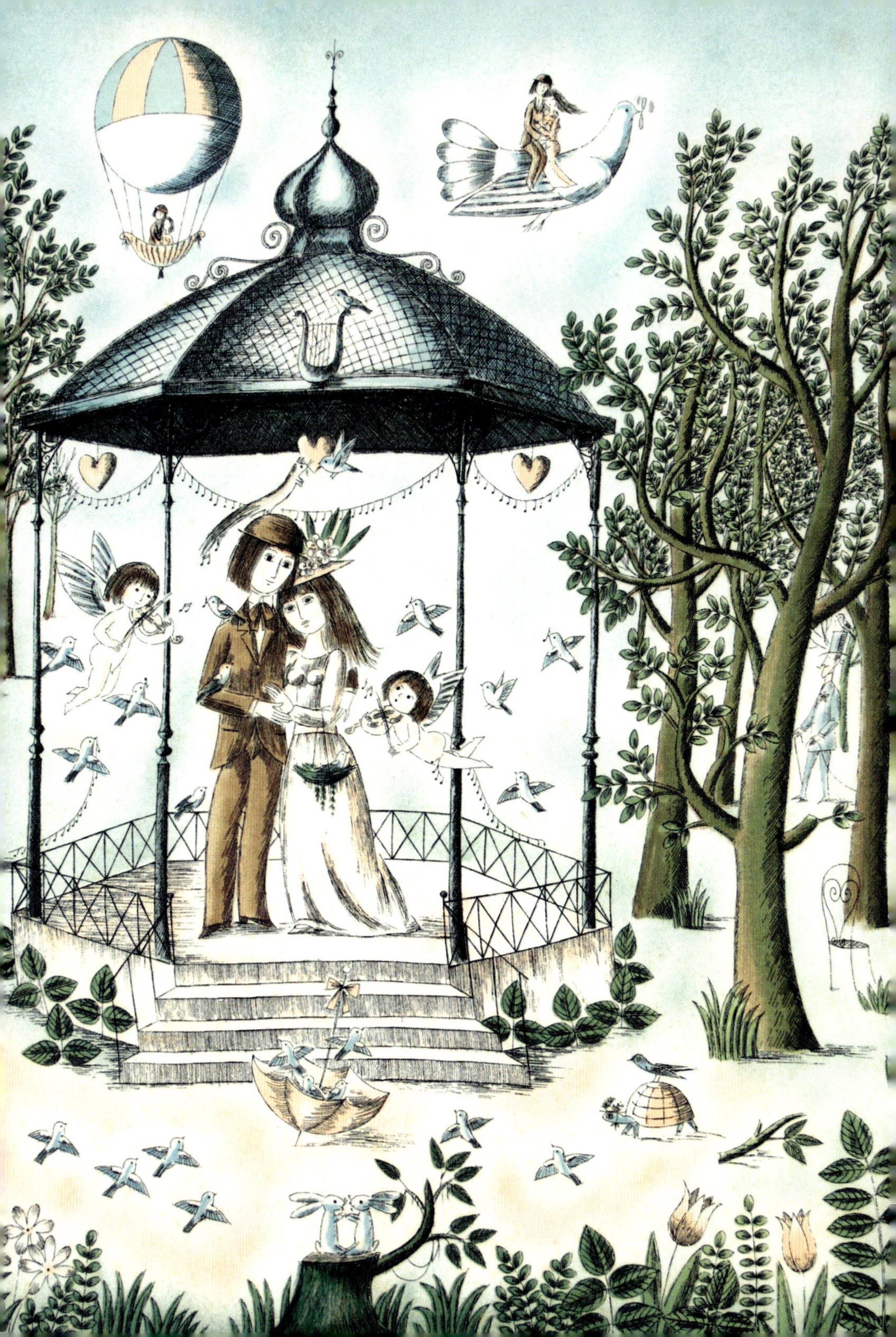

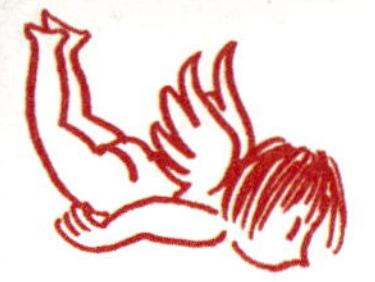

Love beyond reason
Love beyond words
With you as my sole horizon
Time is measured only
By the grief of parting
Love beyond reason.

LOUIS ARAGON
"Love Beyond Reason"

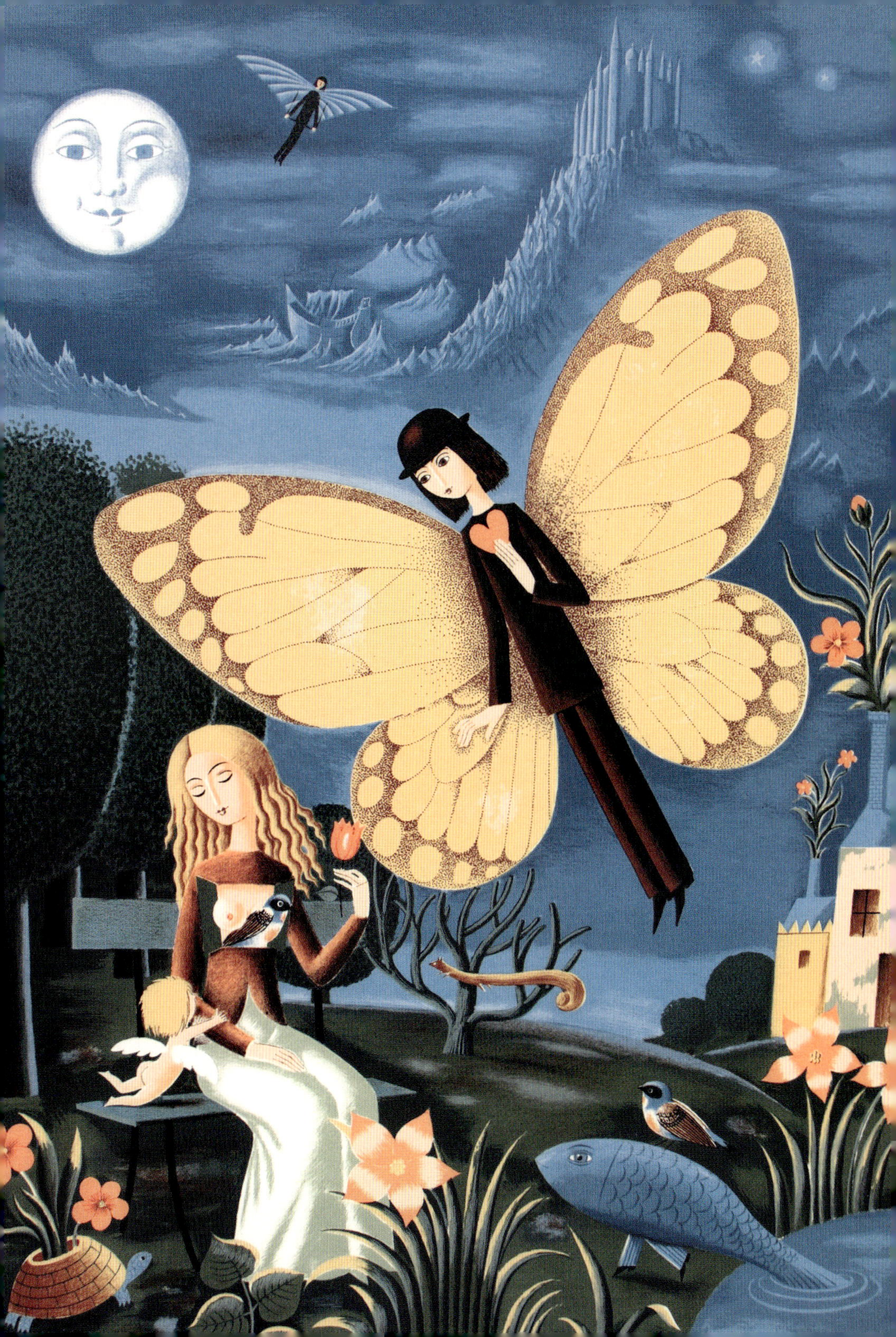

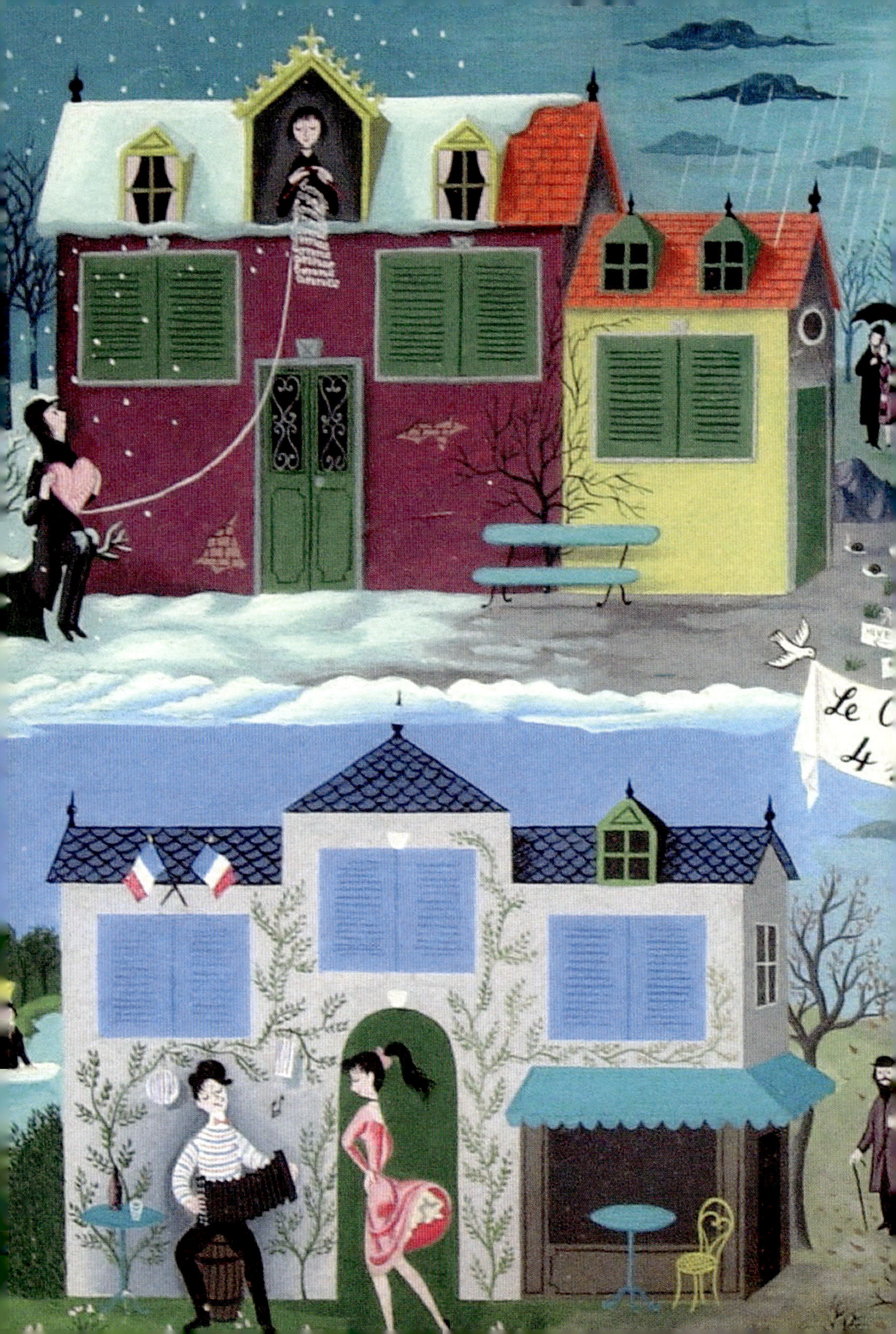

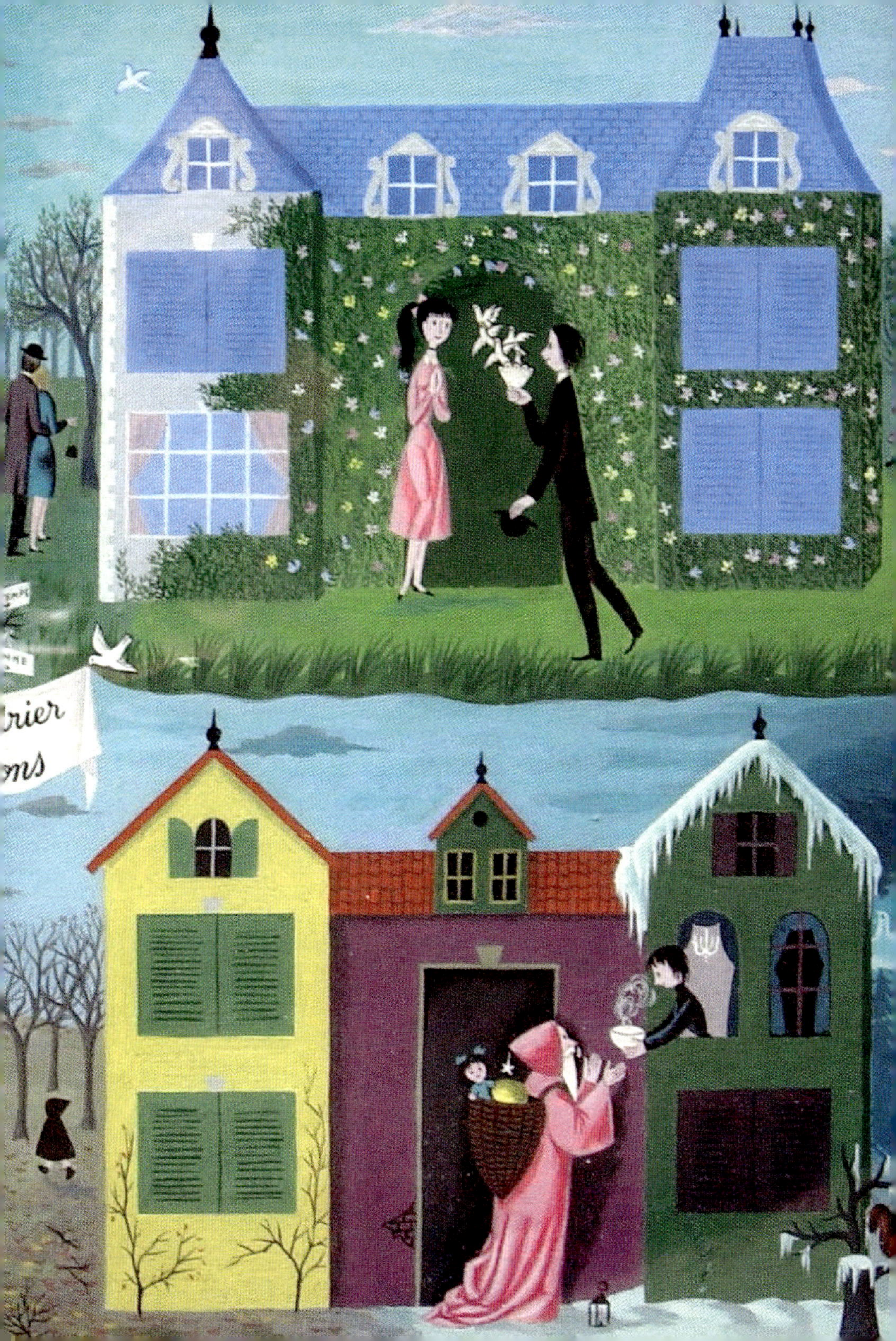
rier
ons

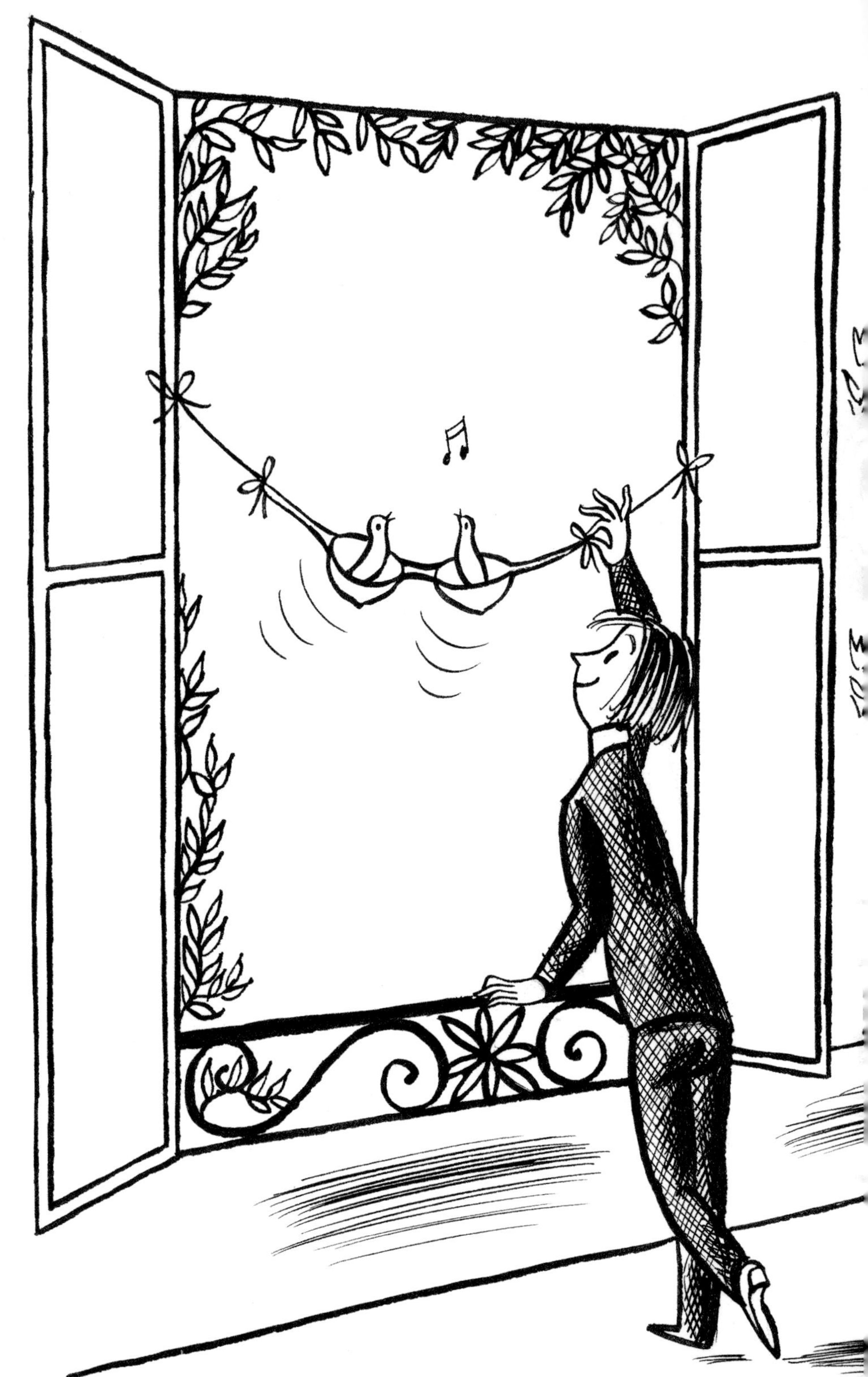

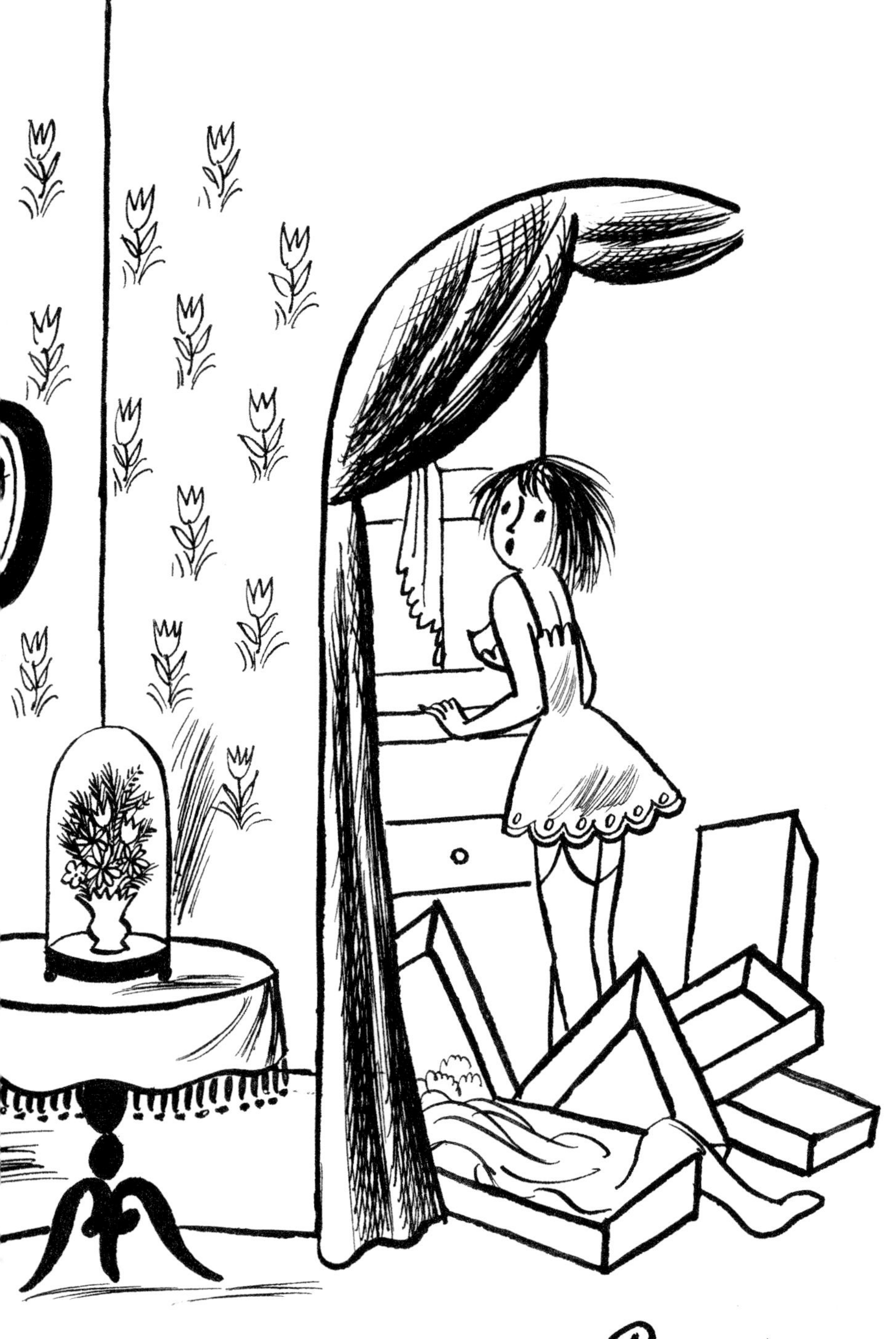
Peynet

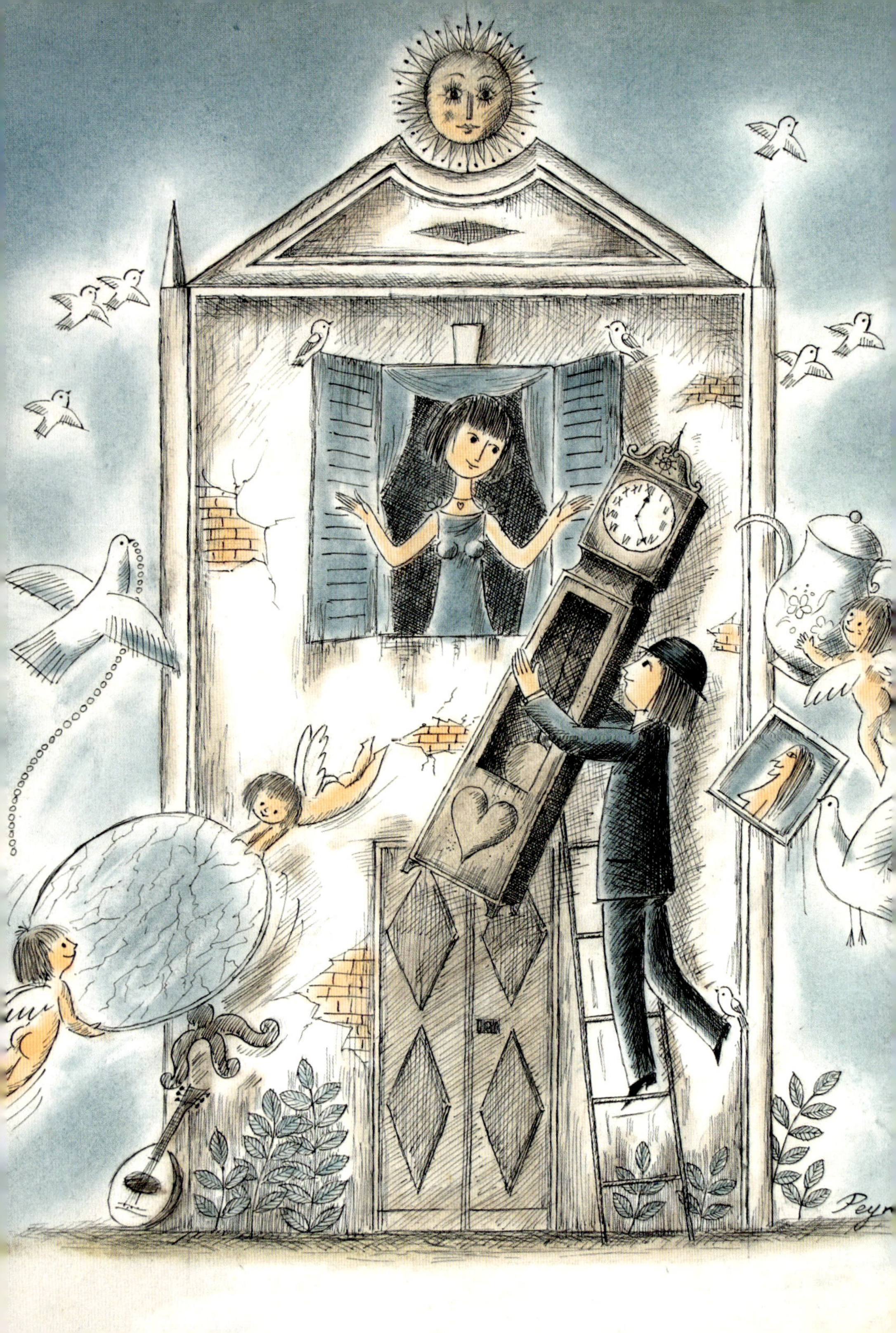

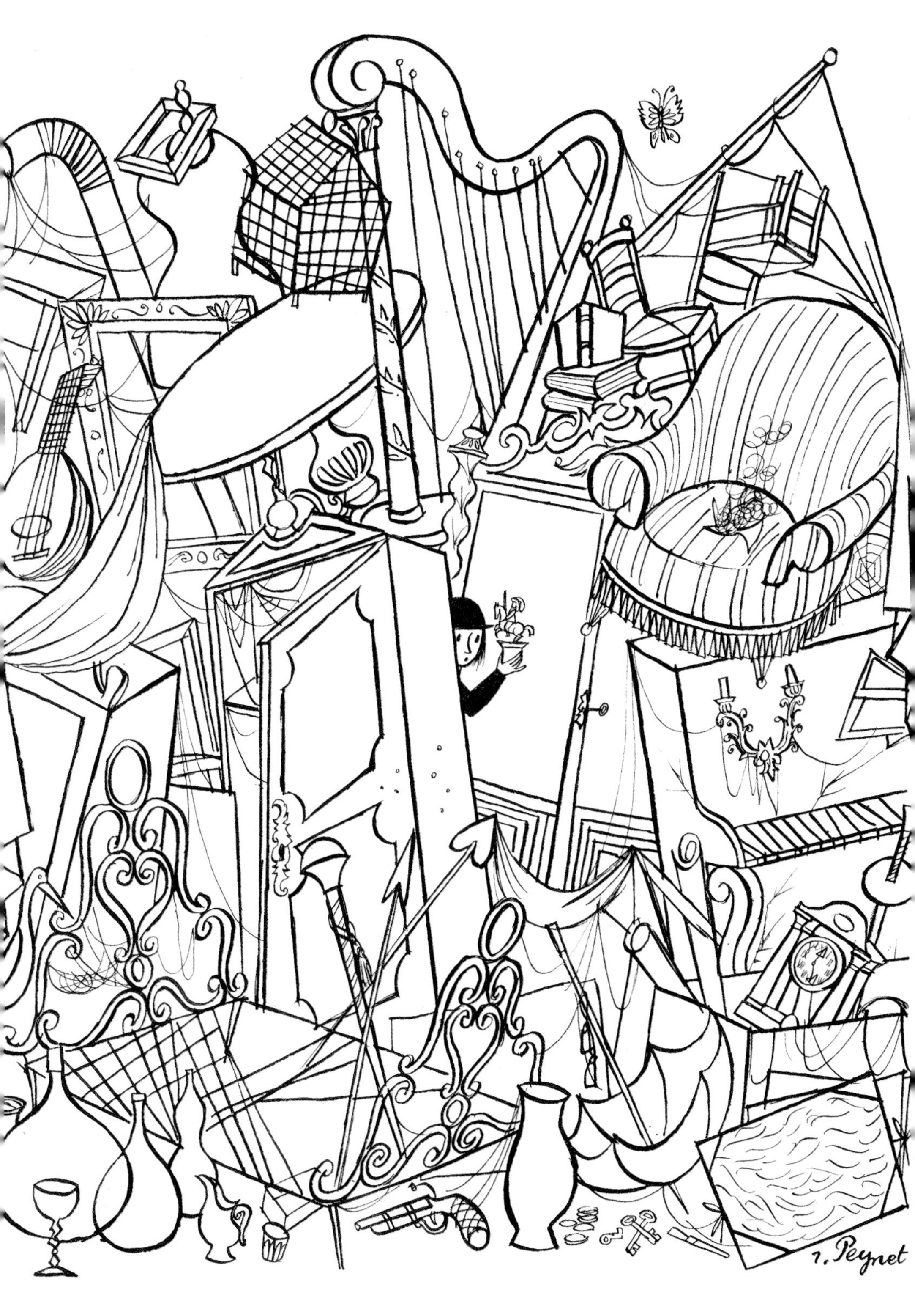
r. Peynet

Lovers who kiss on park benches,
Park benches, park benches,
Are indifferent to
The sidelong glances
Of bystanders
Lovers who kiss on park benches,
Park benches, park benches,
Earnestly declaring “I love you”
To each other have sweet
little faces.

GEORGES BRASSENS
“Park Benches”

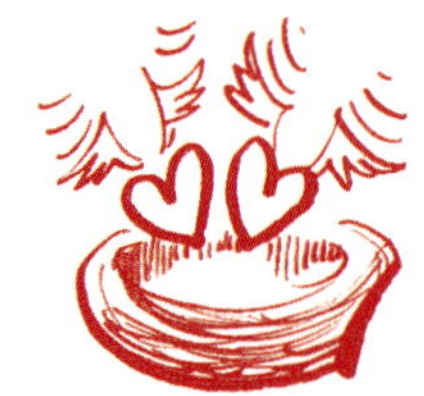

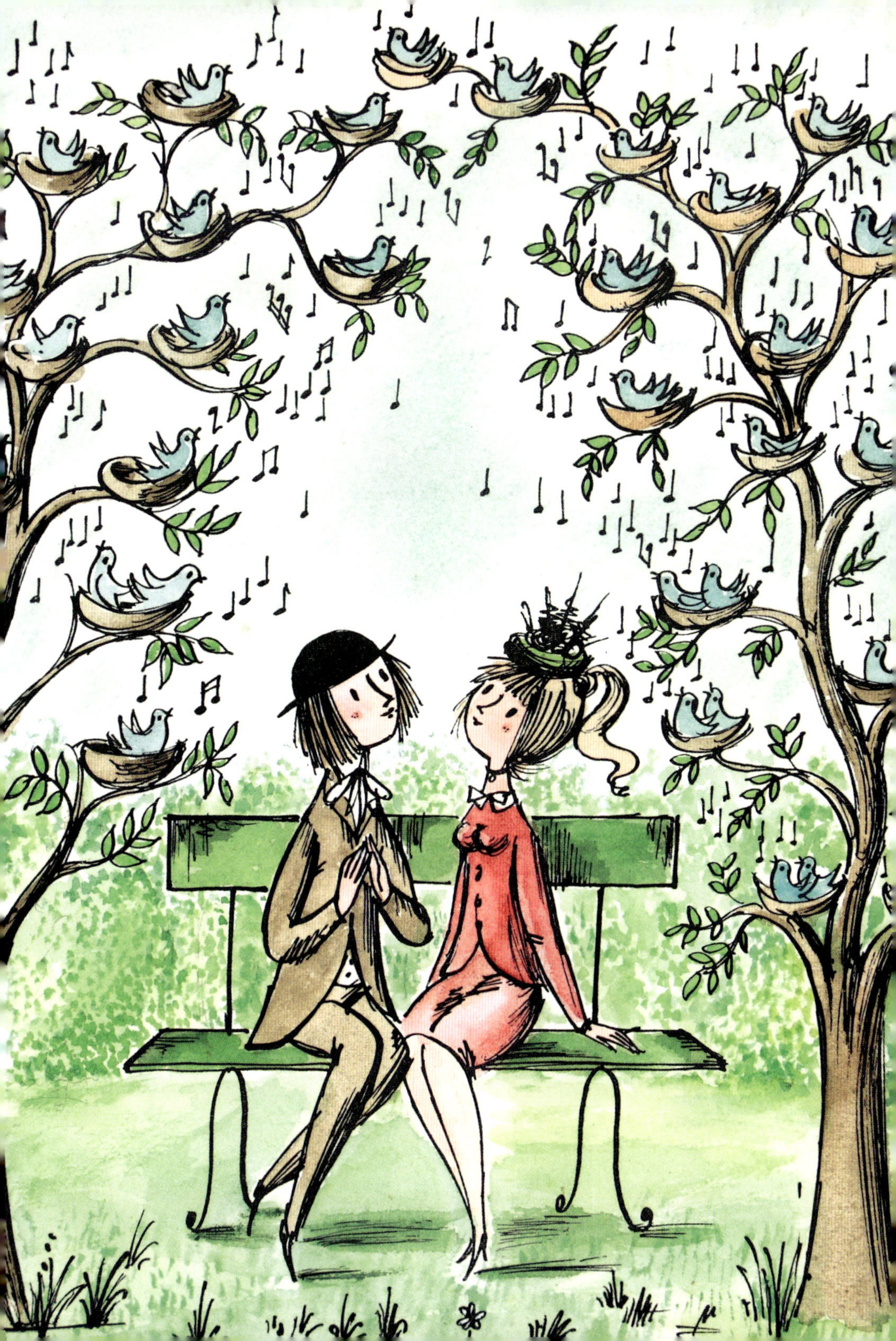

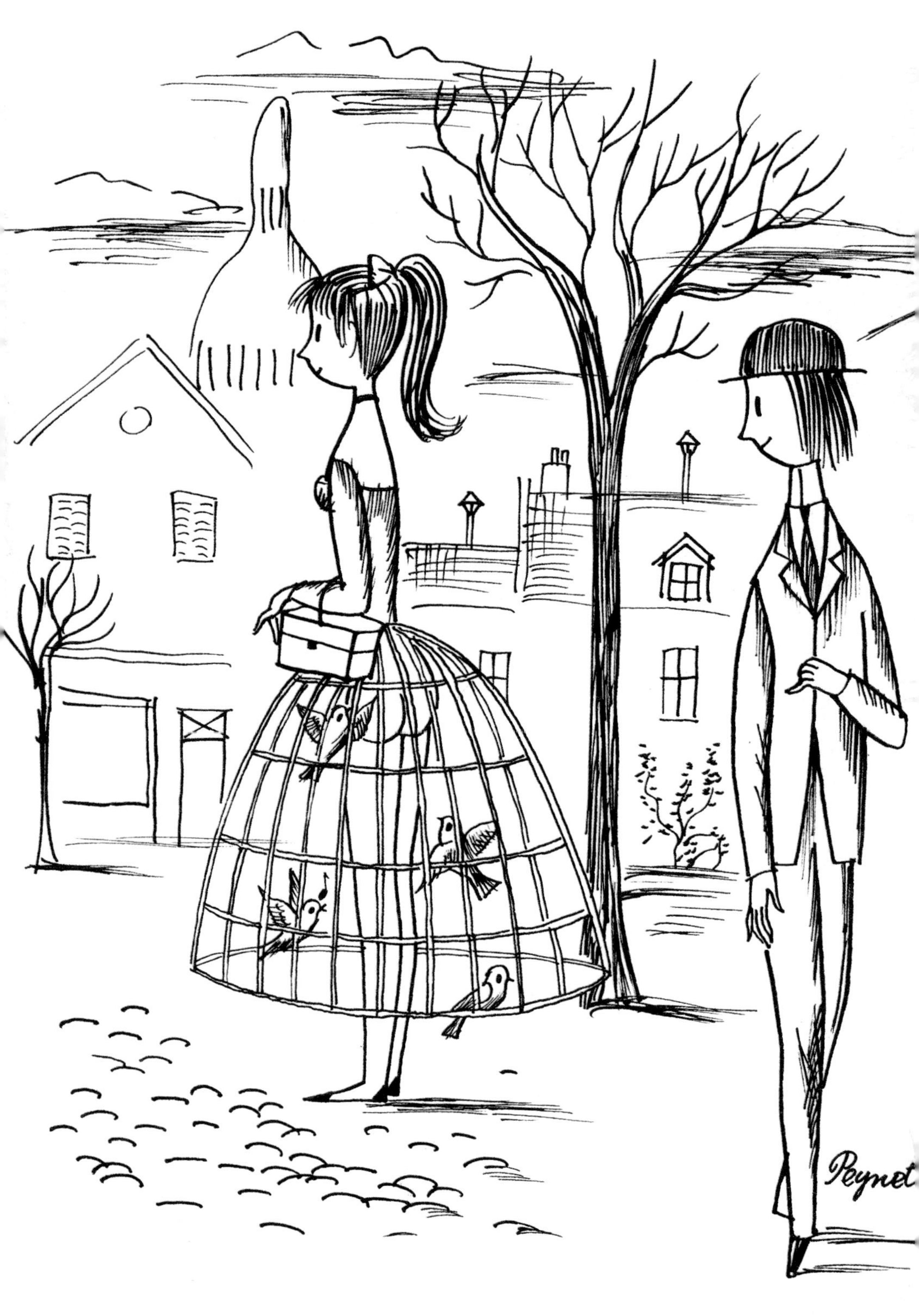
Peynet

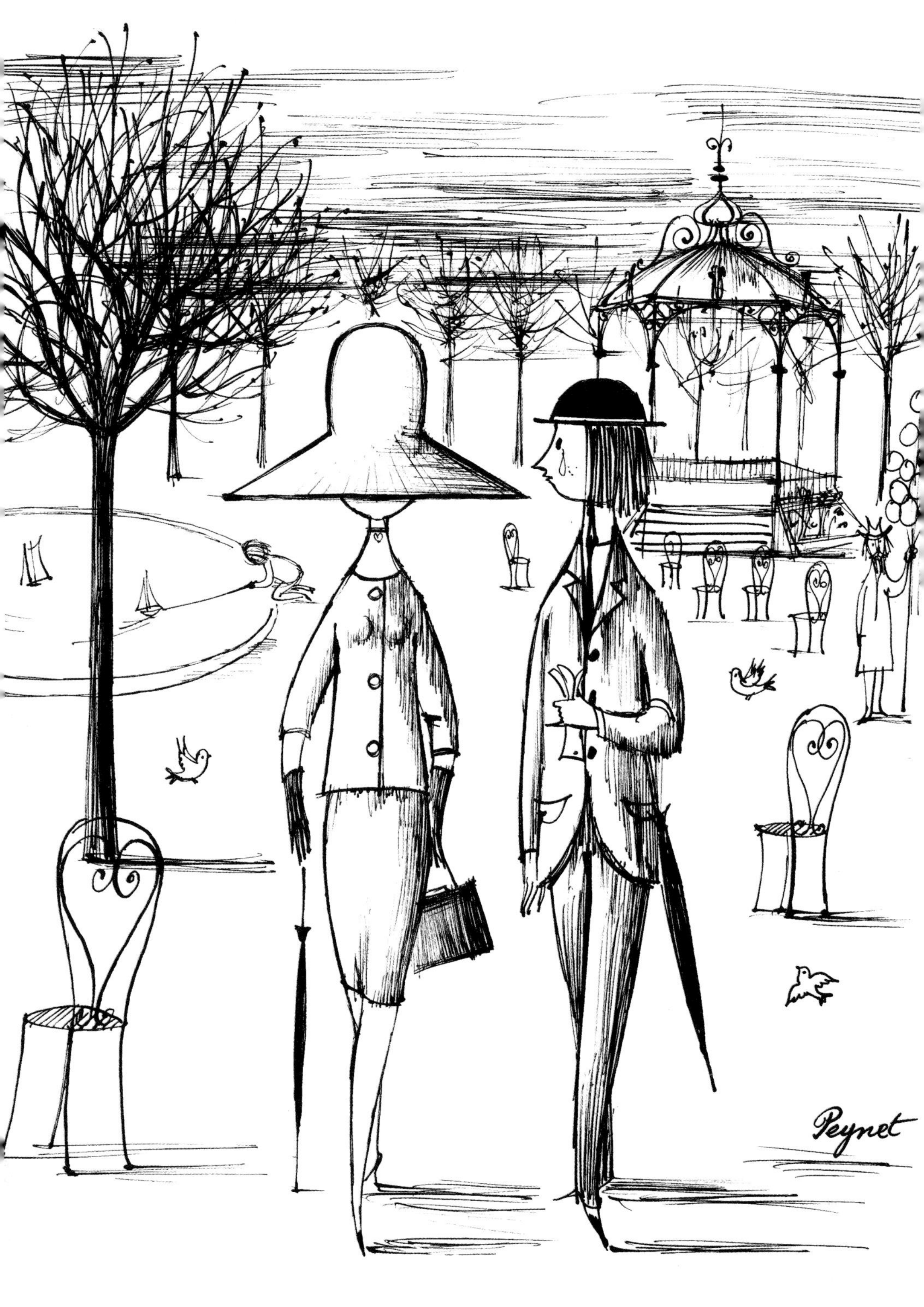
Peynet

To be in love
is to be amazed.
When amazement
fades, it's over.

FRÉDÉRIC BEIGBEDER
The Romantic Egoist

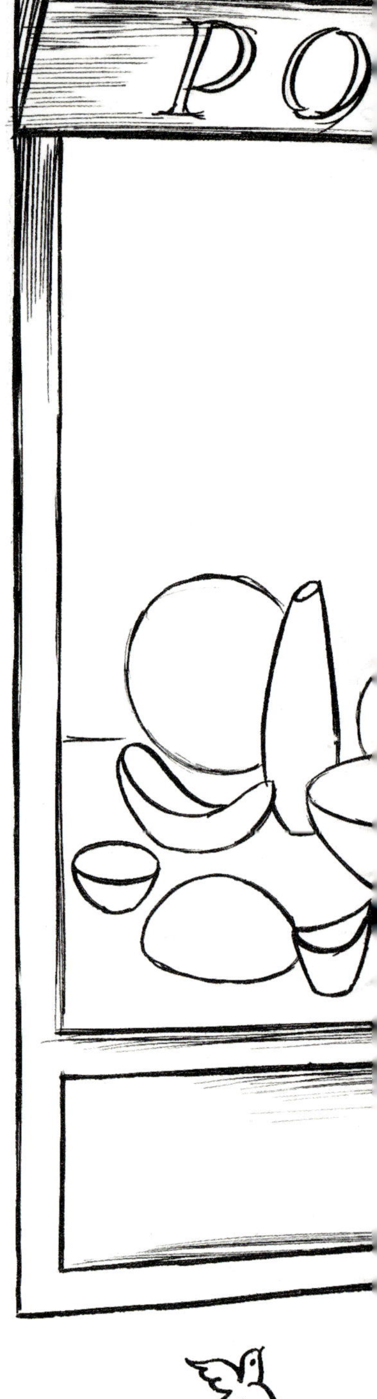

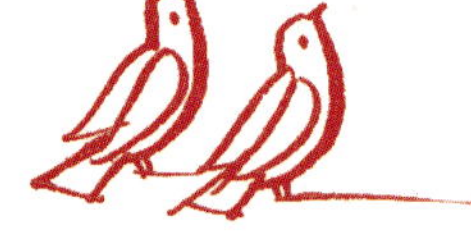

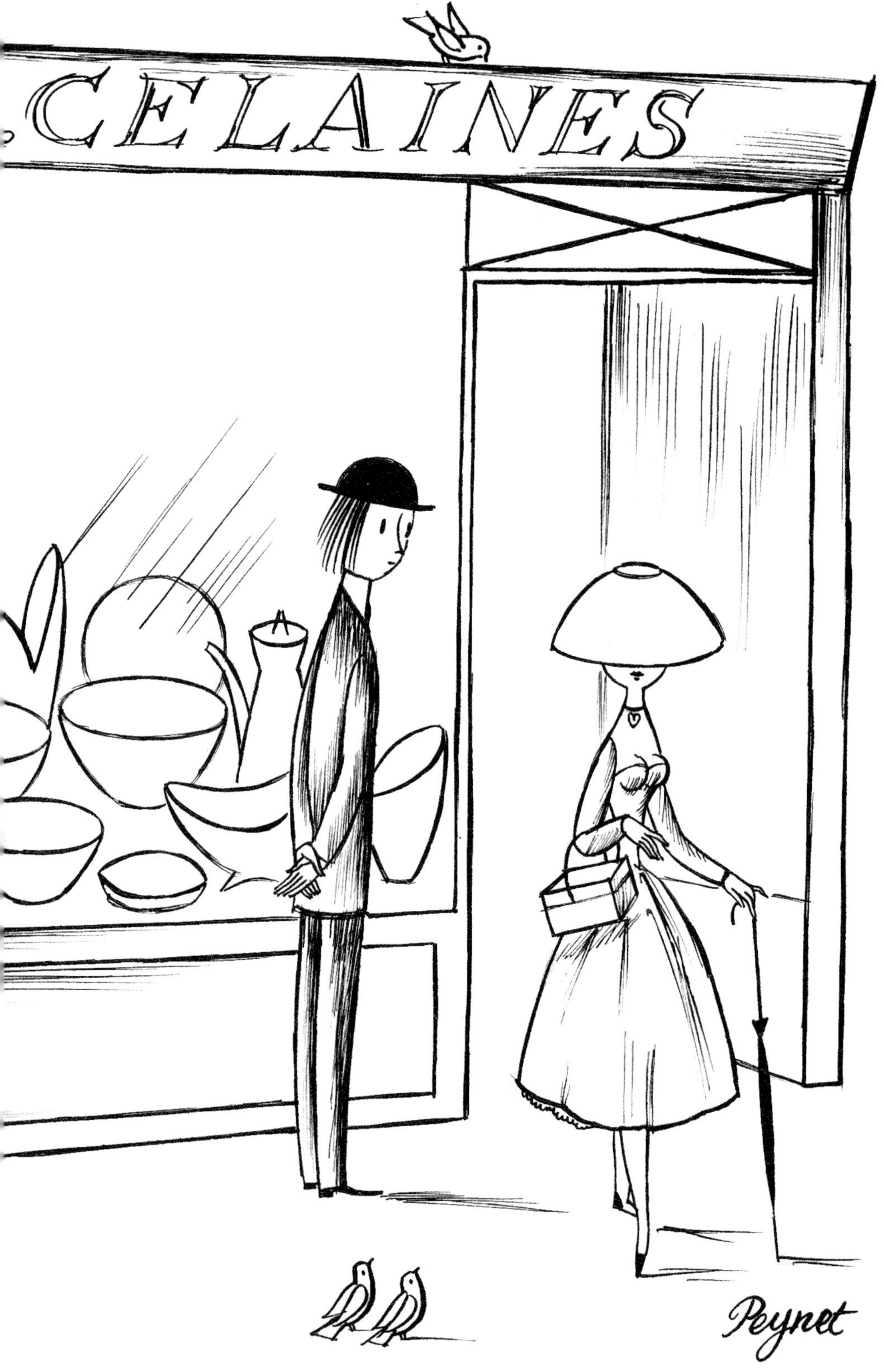
CELAINES
Peynet

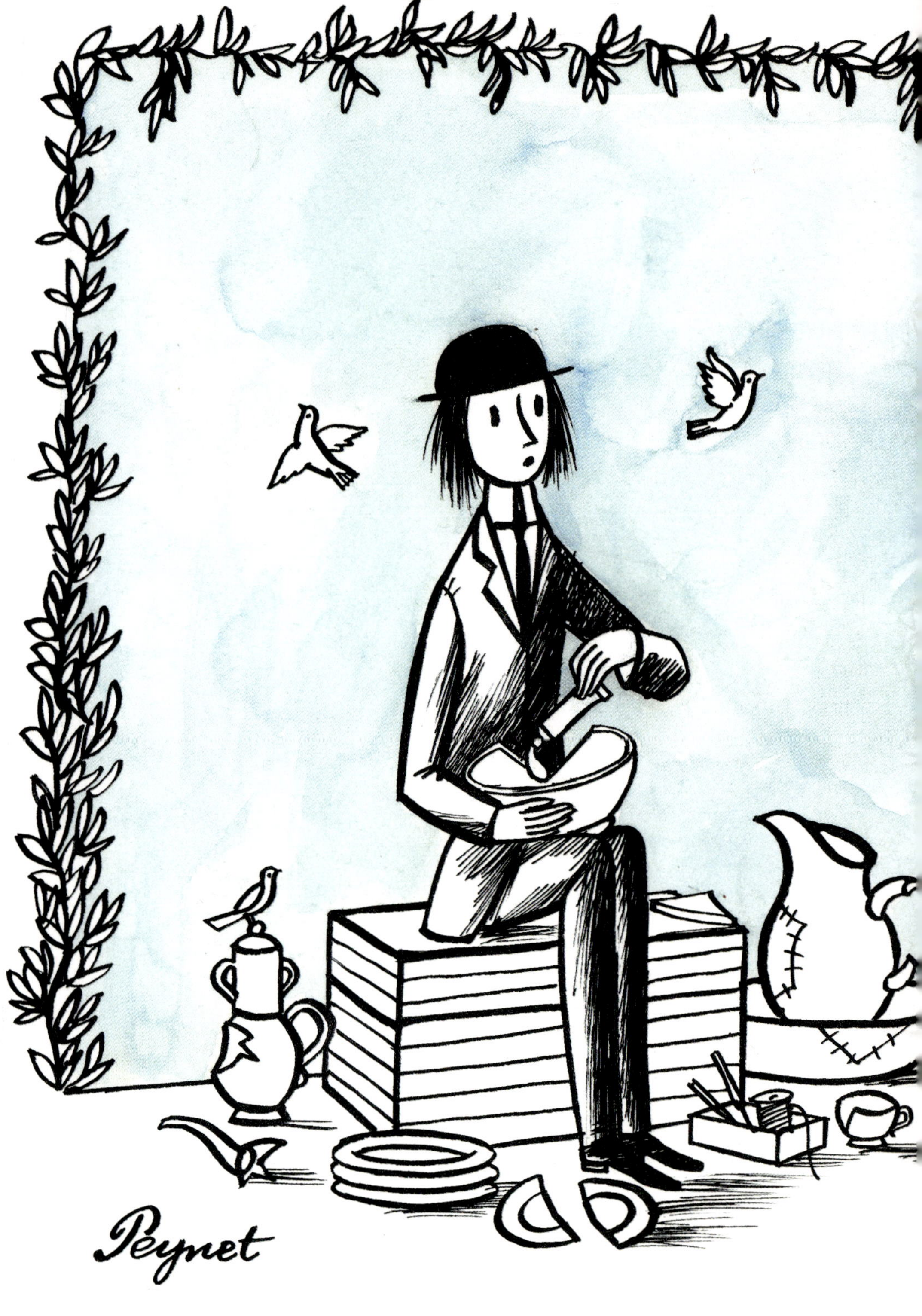
Peynet

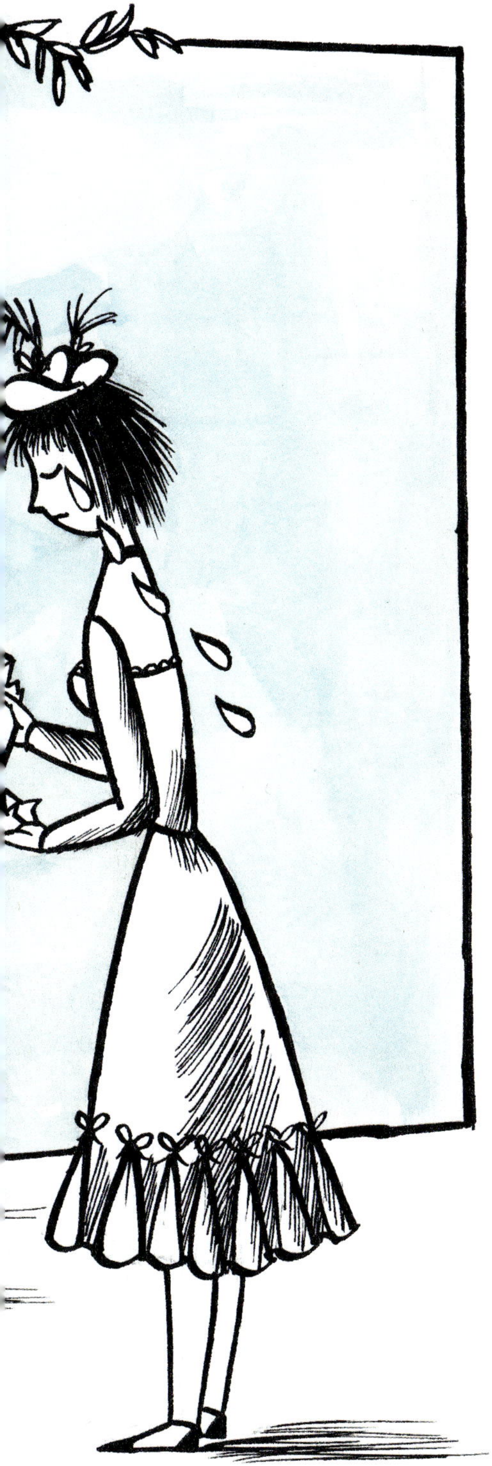

Only love
can heal
the wounds
of love.

Anne Dandurand
Heartbreak

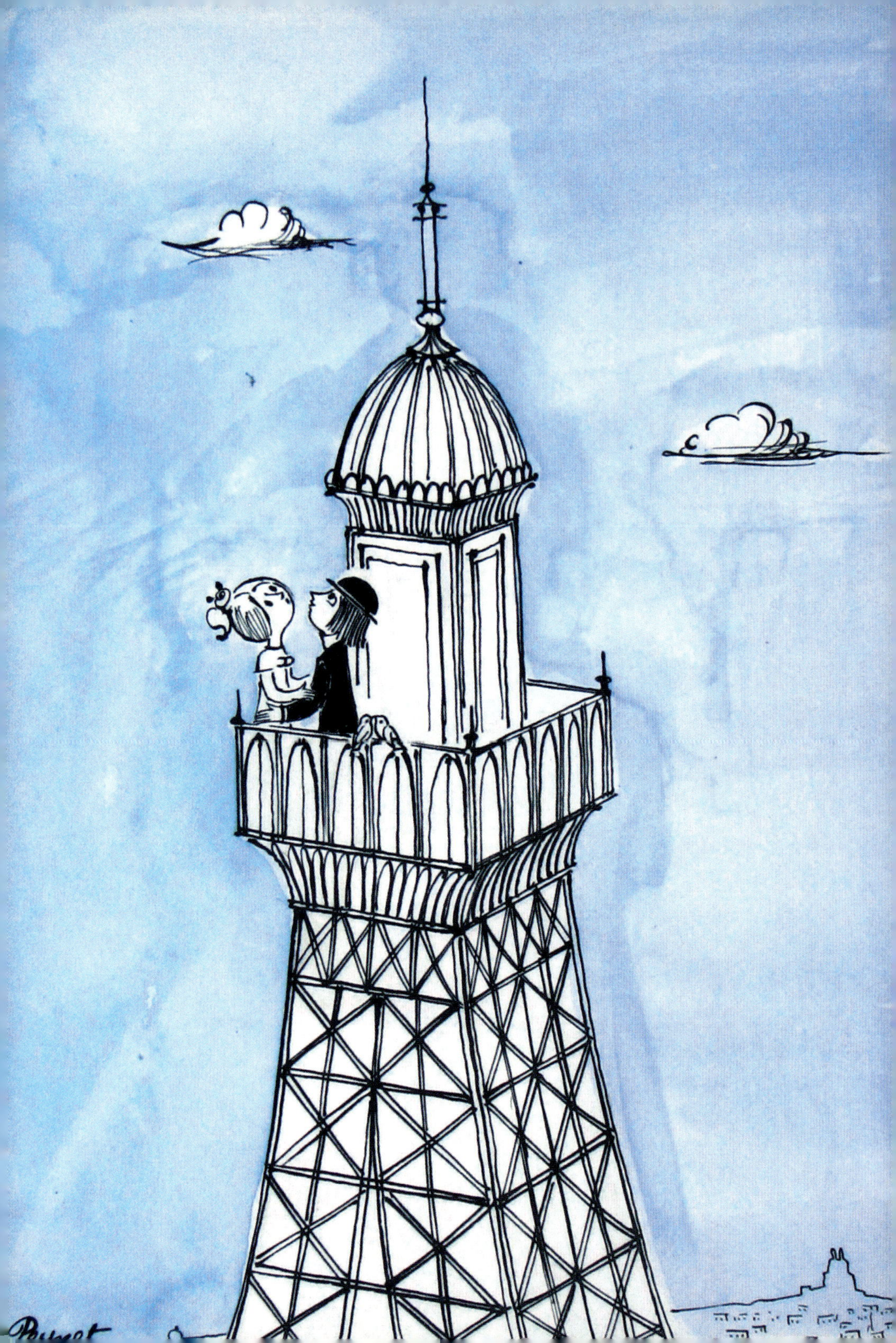

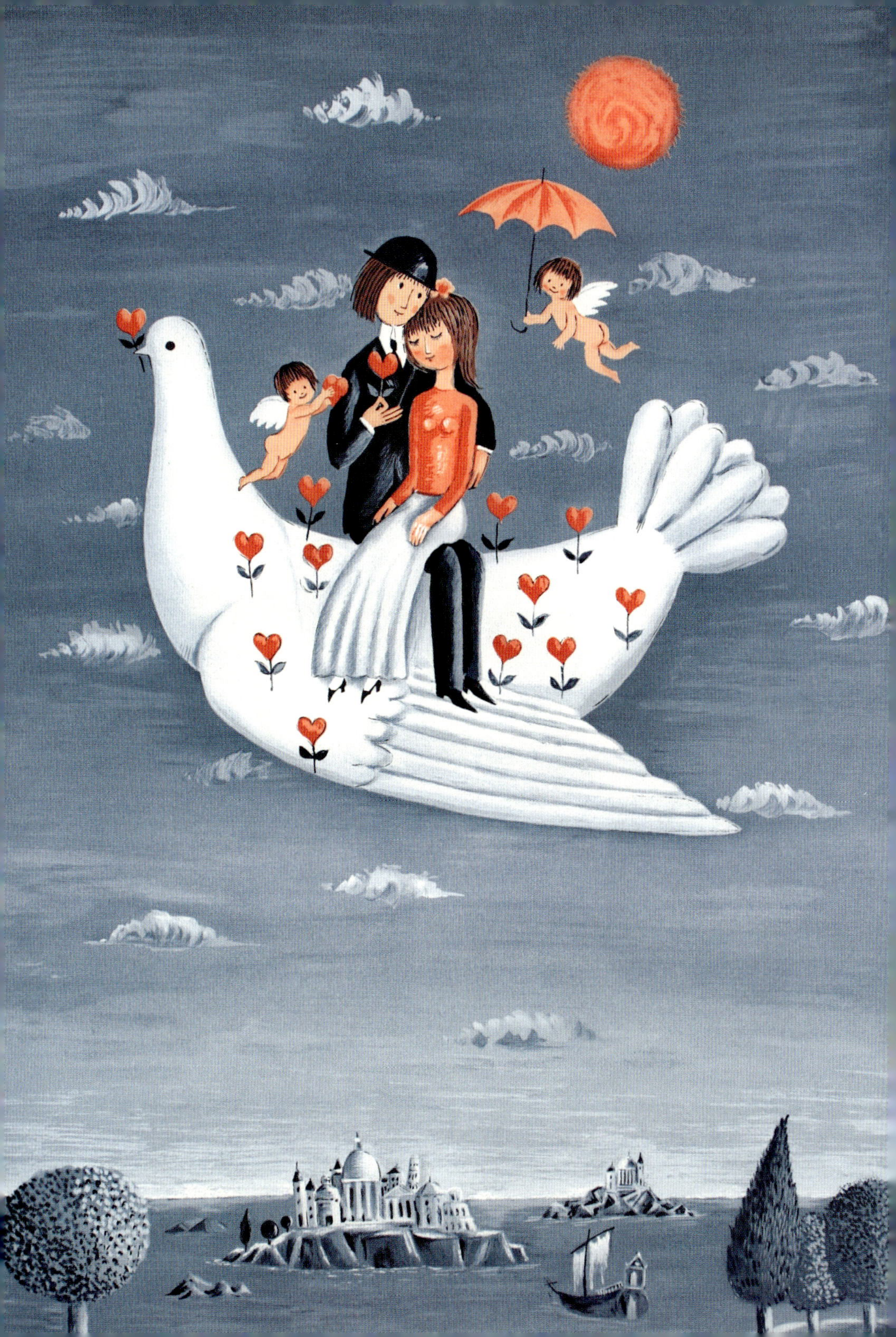

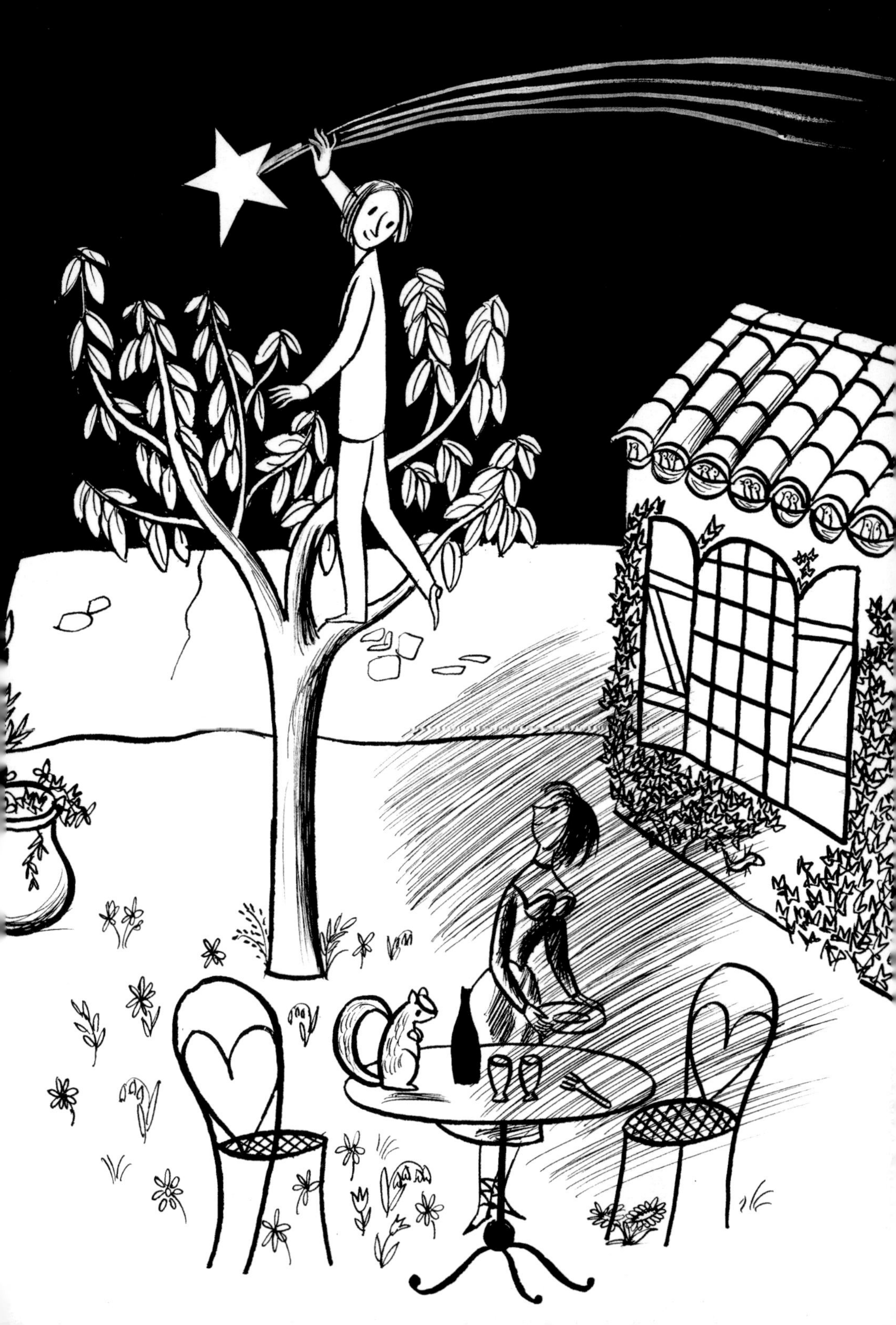

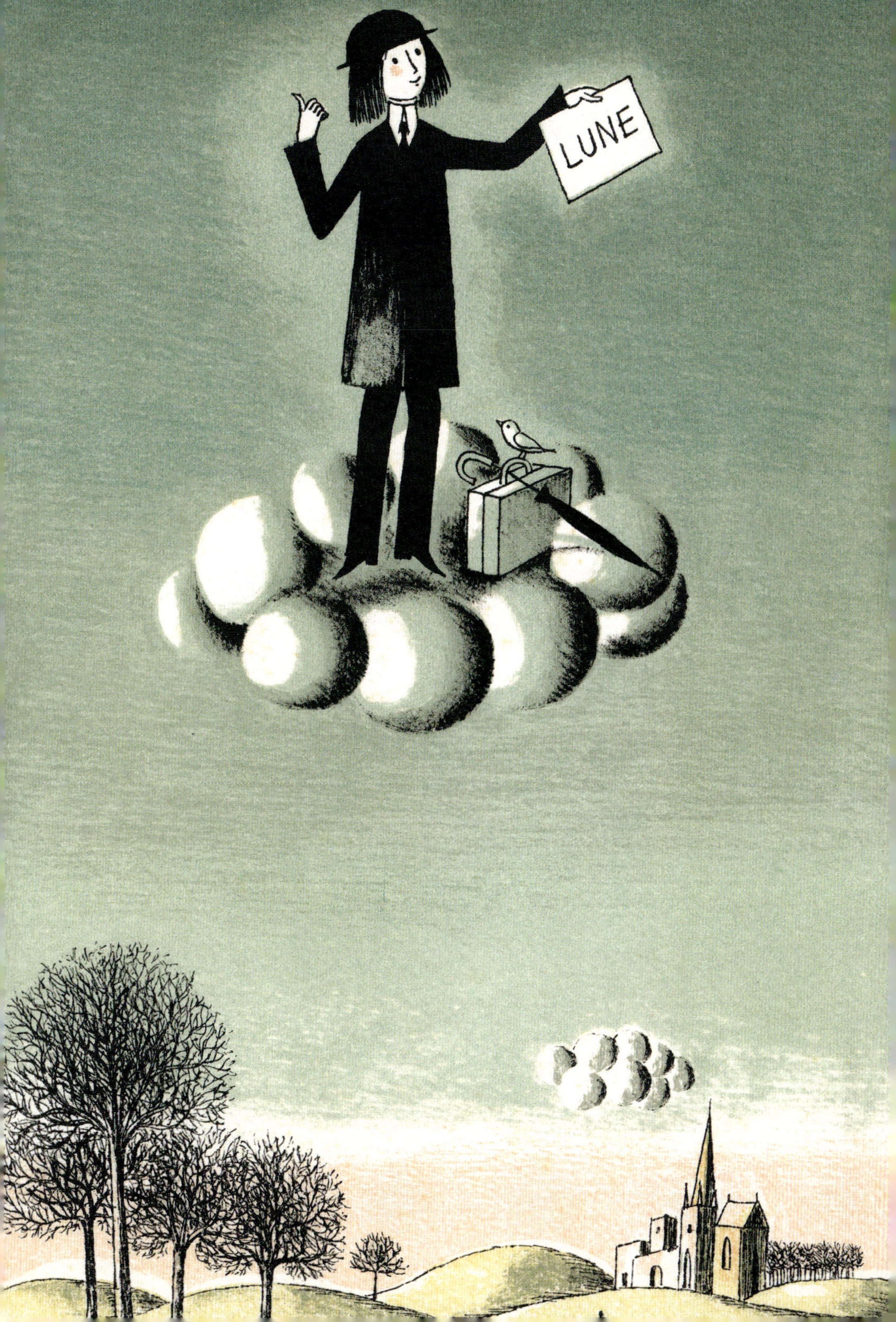
LUNE

You make my head spin
My very own carousel
The ride never ends
When you hold me in your arms

I could fly around the world
And never feel this way
It could never spin fast enough
To make me feel the way you do . . .

Édith Piaf
"My Very Own Carousel"

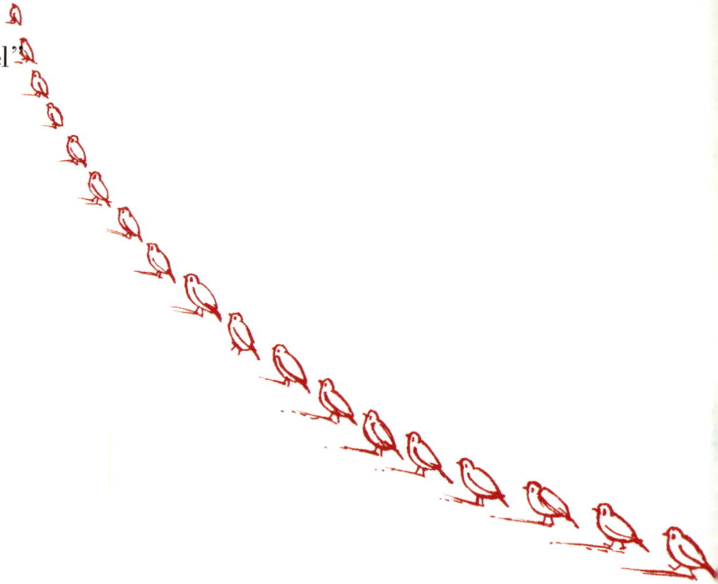

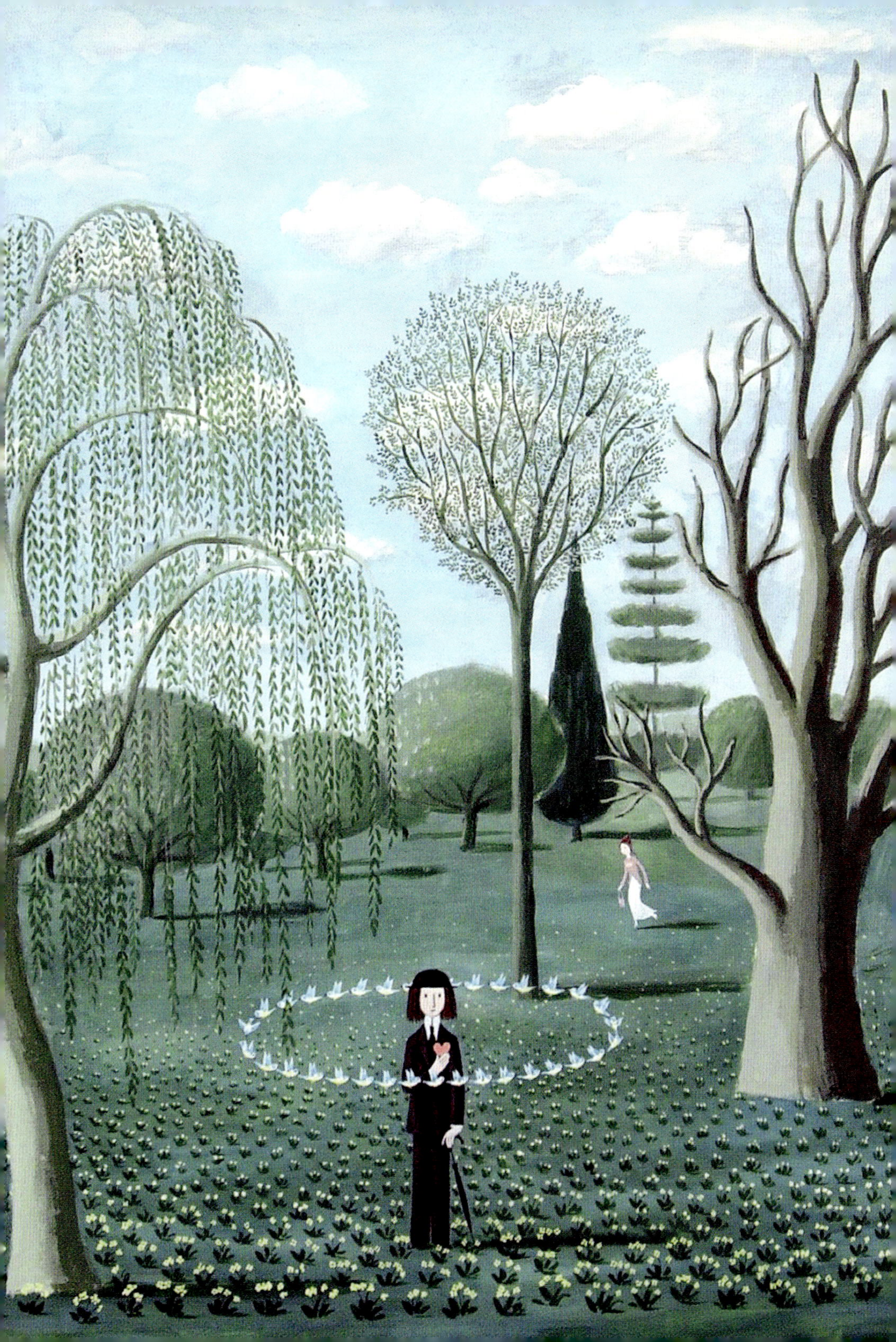

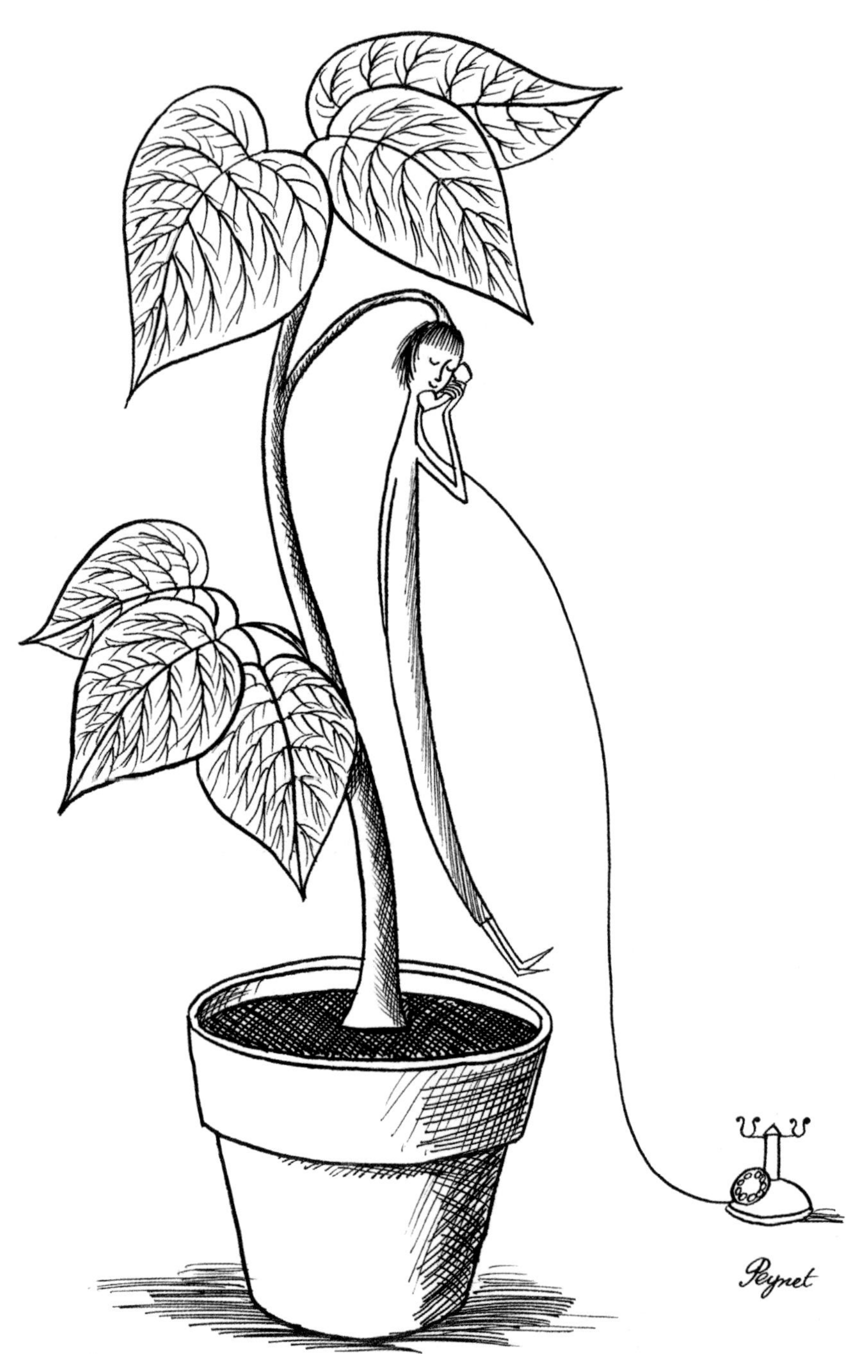
Peynet

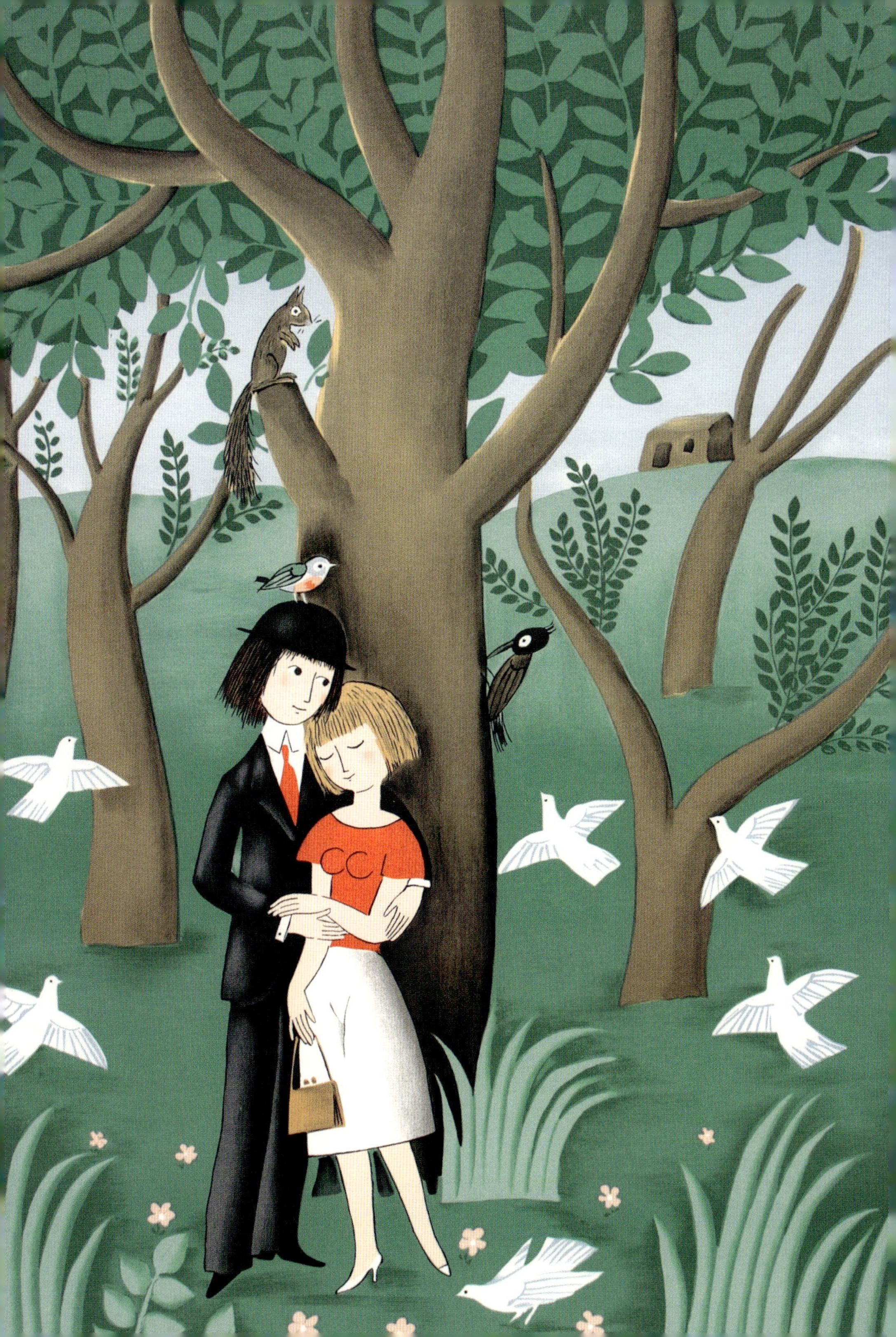

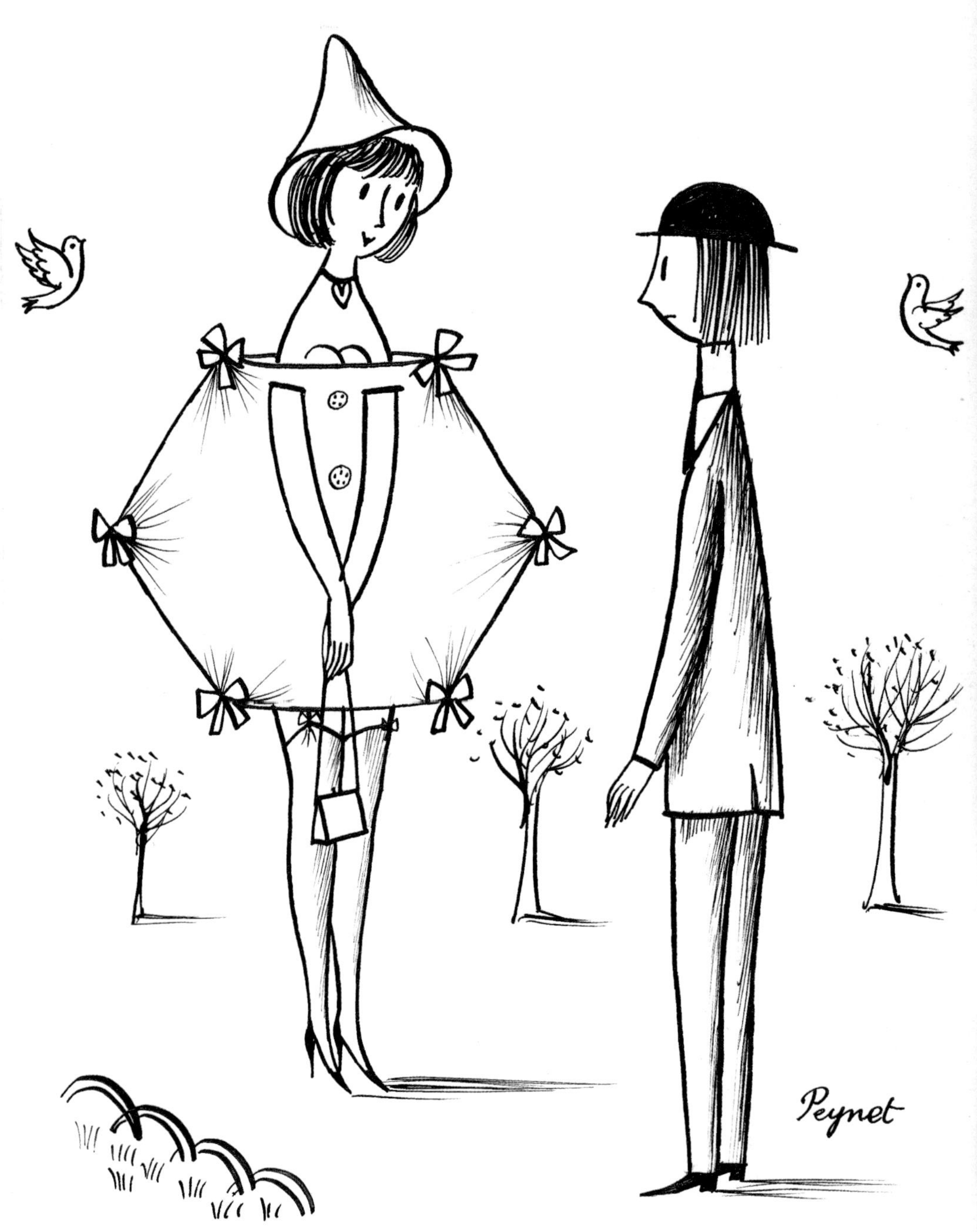
Peynet

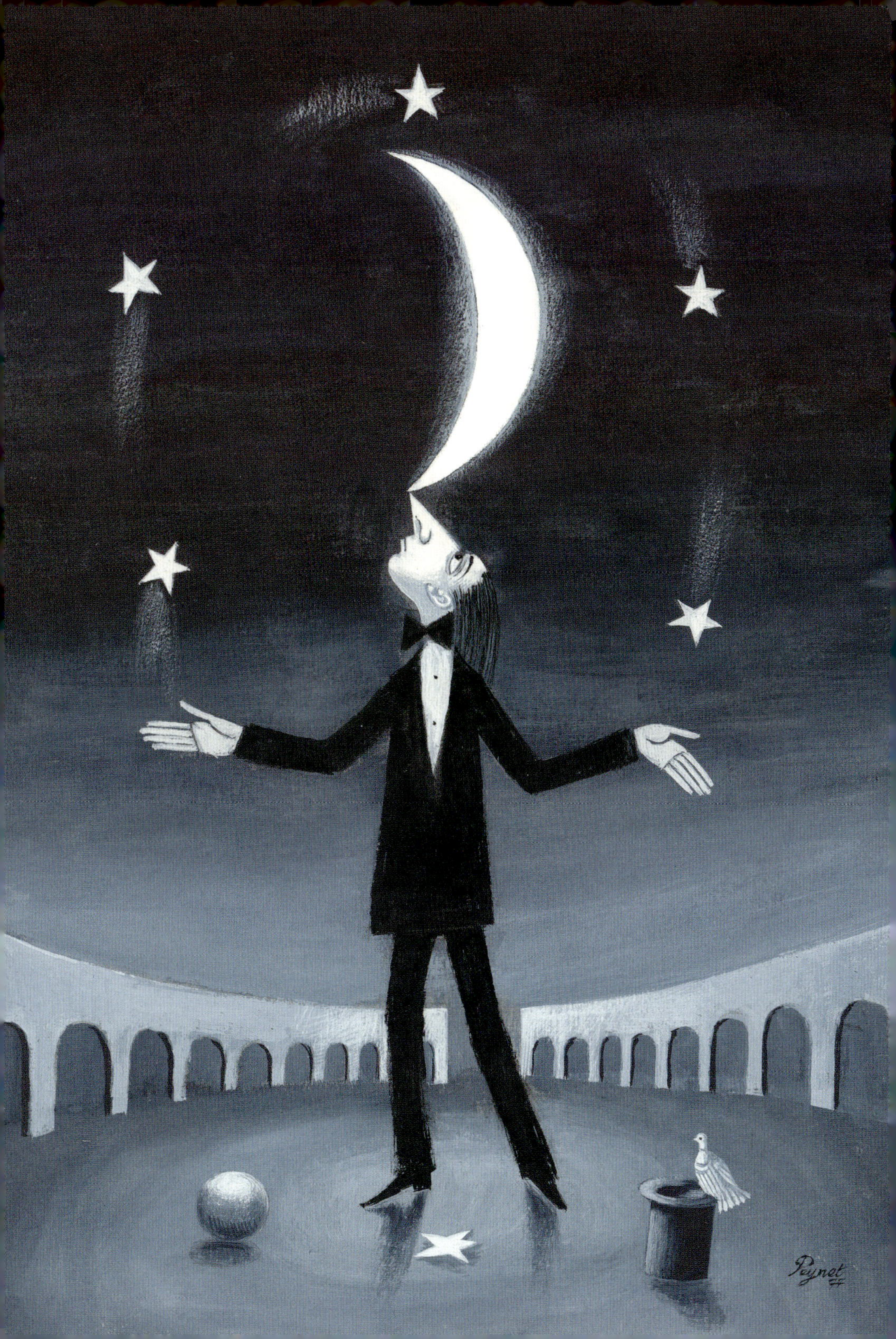
Peynet

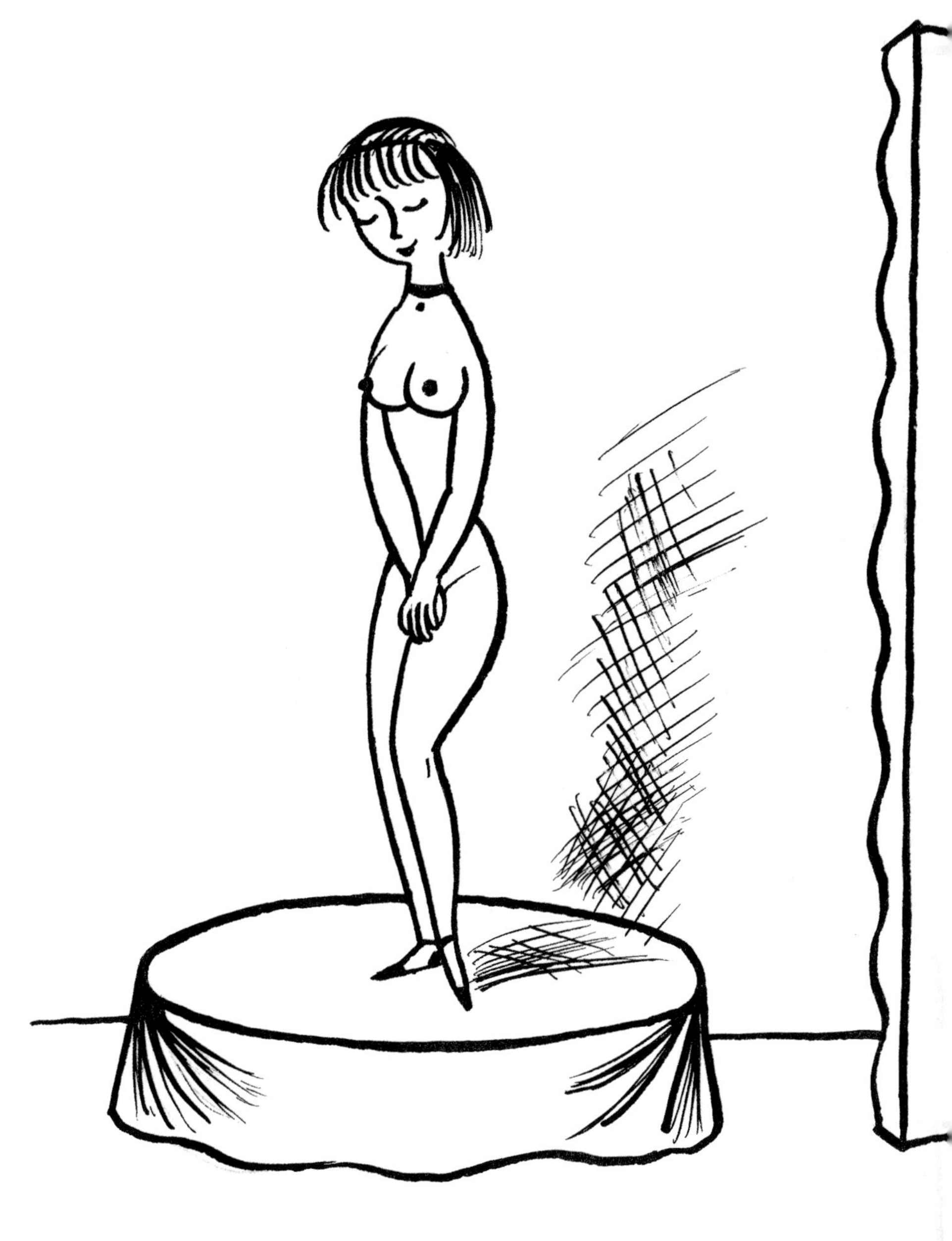
r. Peynet

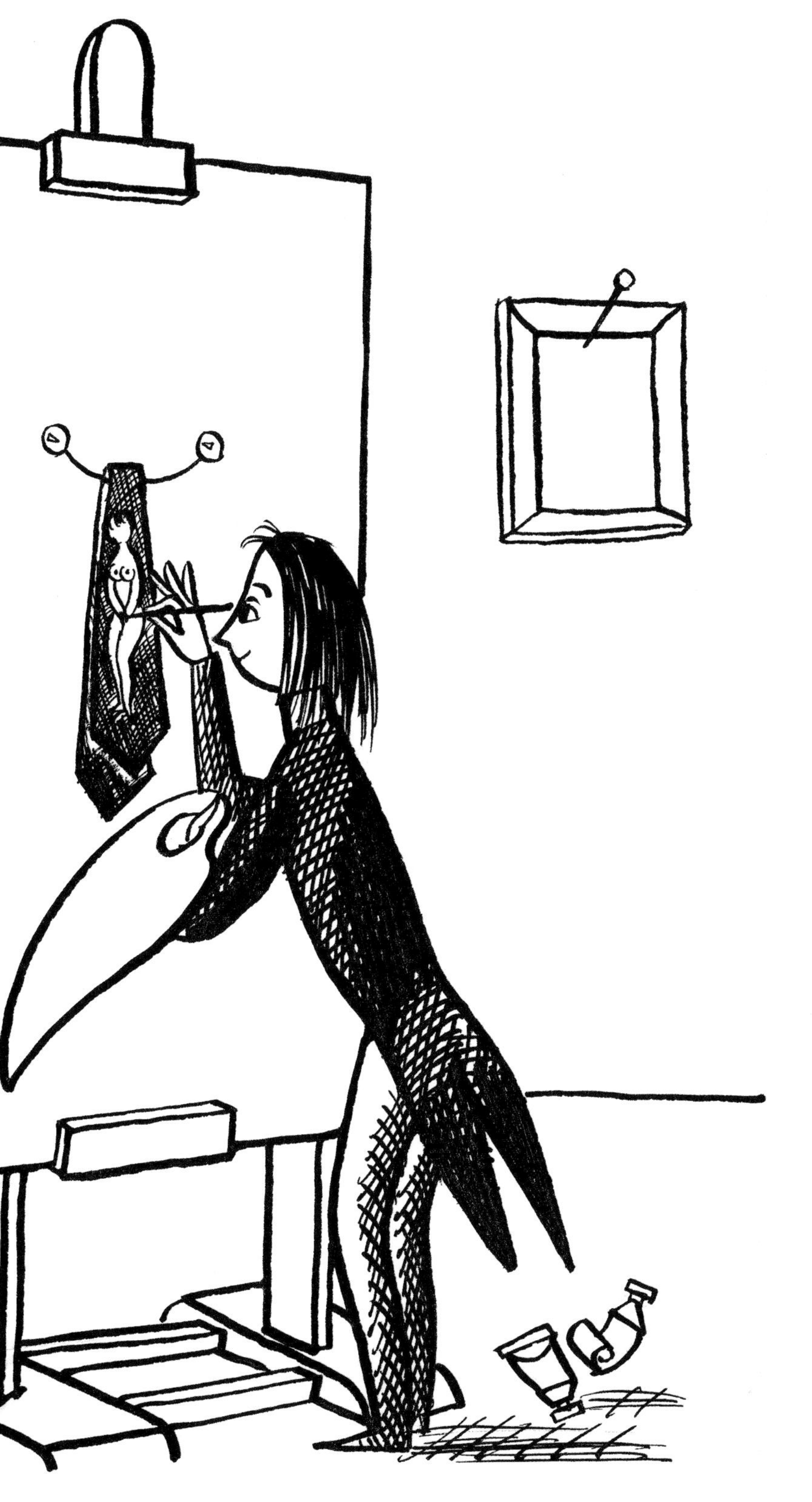

I received a letter
About a month ago
That was not addressed to me
The mailman's error
A perfumed message
Marked with crimson lipstick
I should perhaps have
Left it unopened.

Renan Luce
"The Letter"

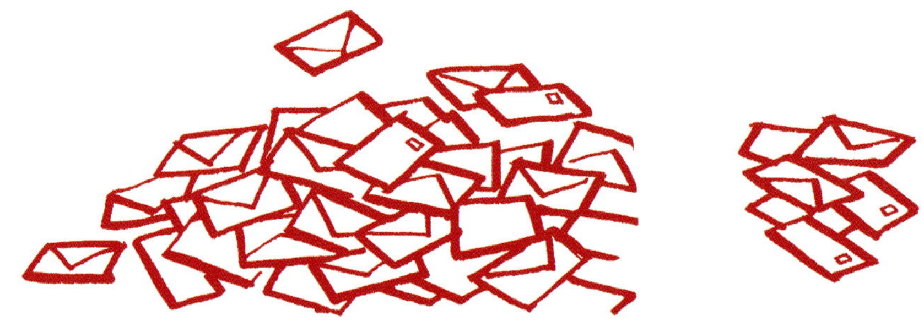

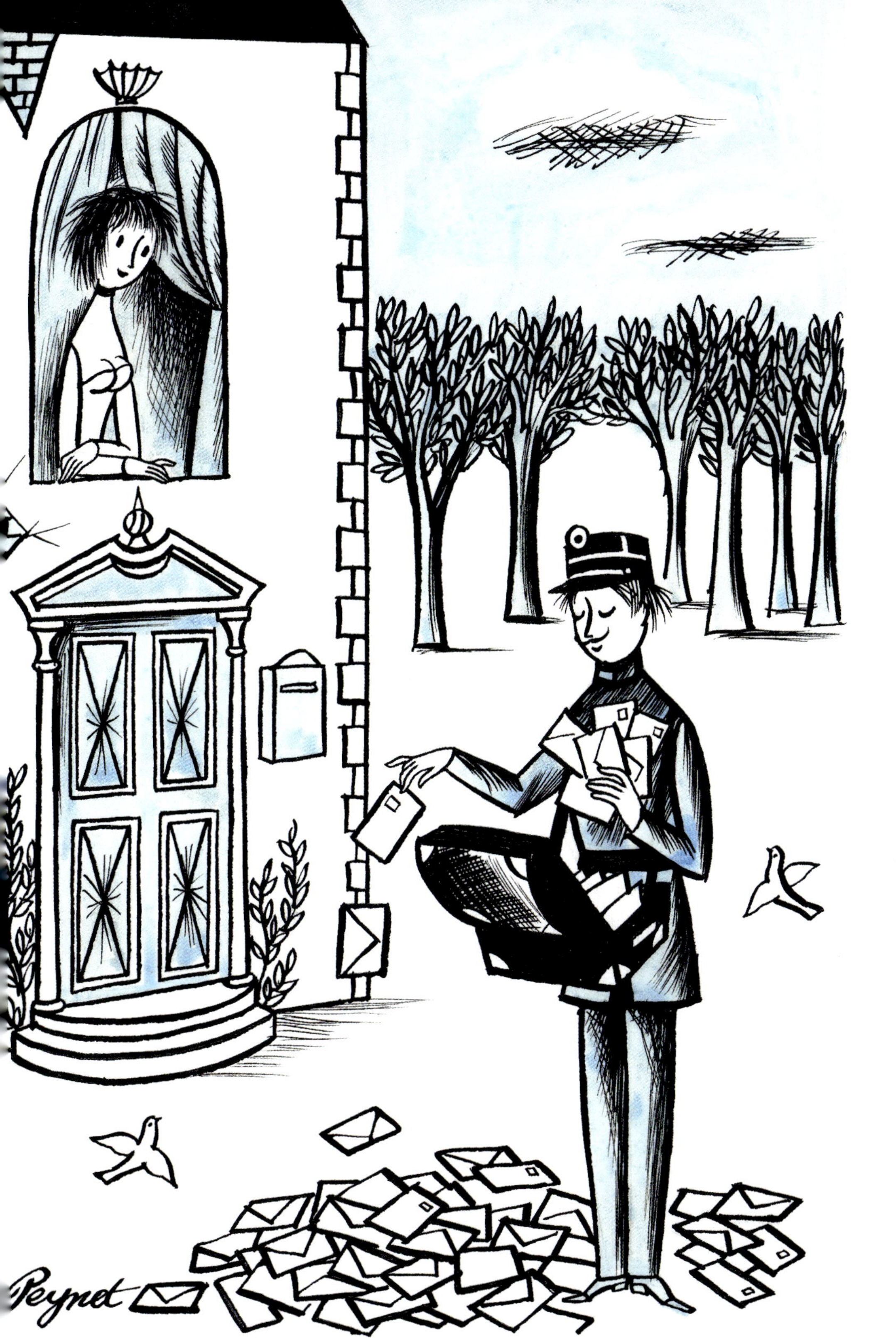
Peynet

Autumn leaves
Are swept away
So too, memories and regrets
But my silent and
Faithful love
Endures and cherishes life
I loved you so, you were so beautiful

JACQUES PRÉVERT
"Autumn Leaves"

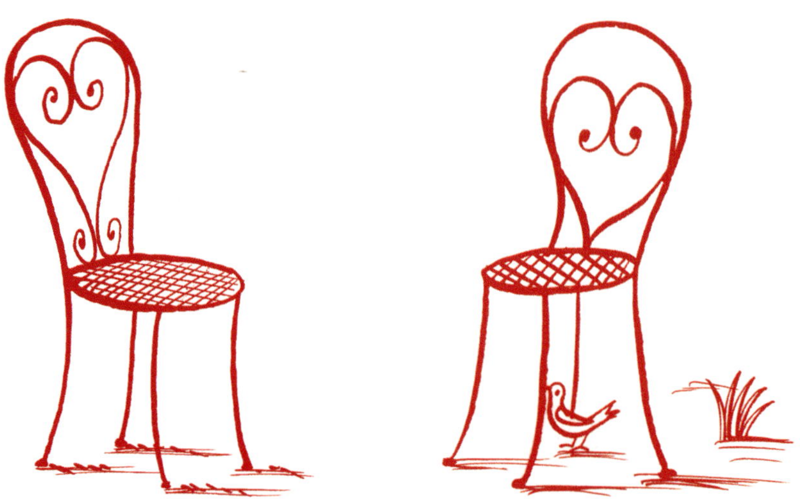

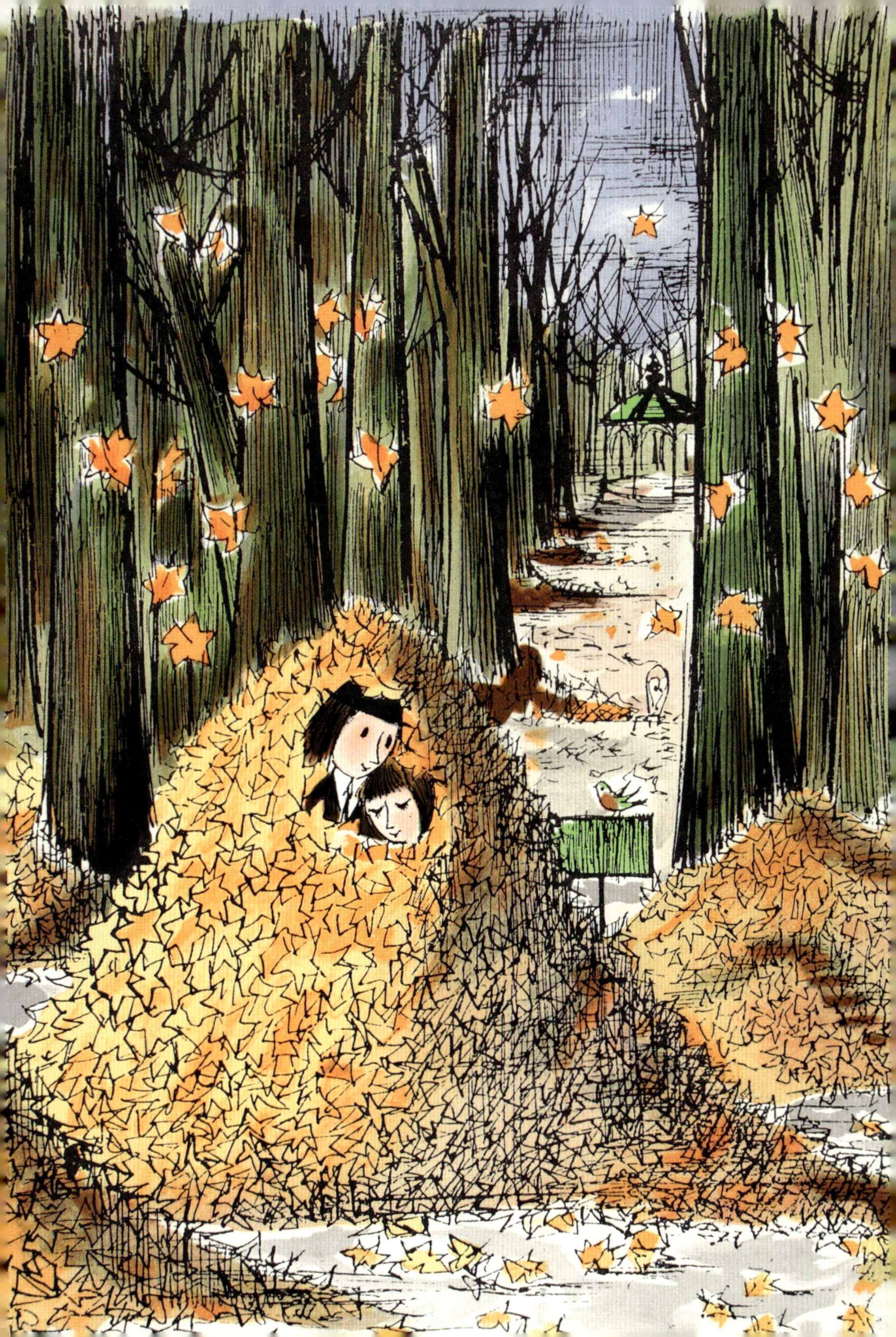

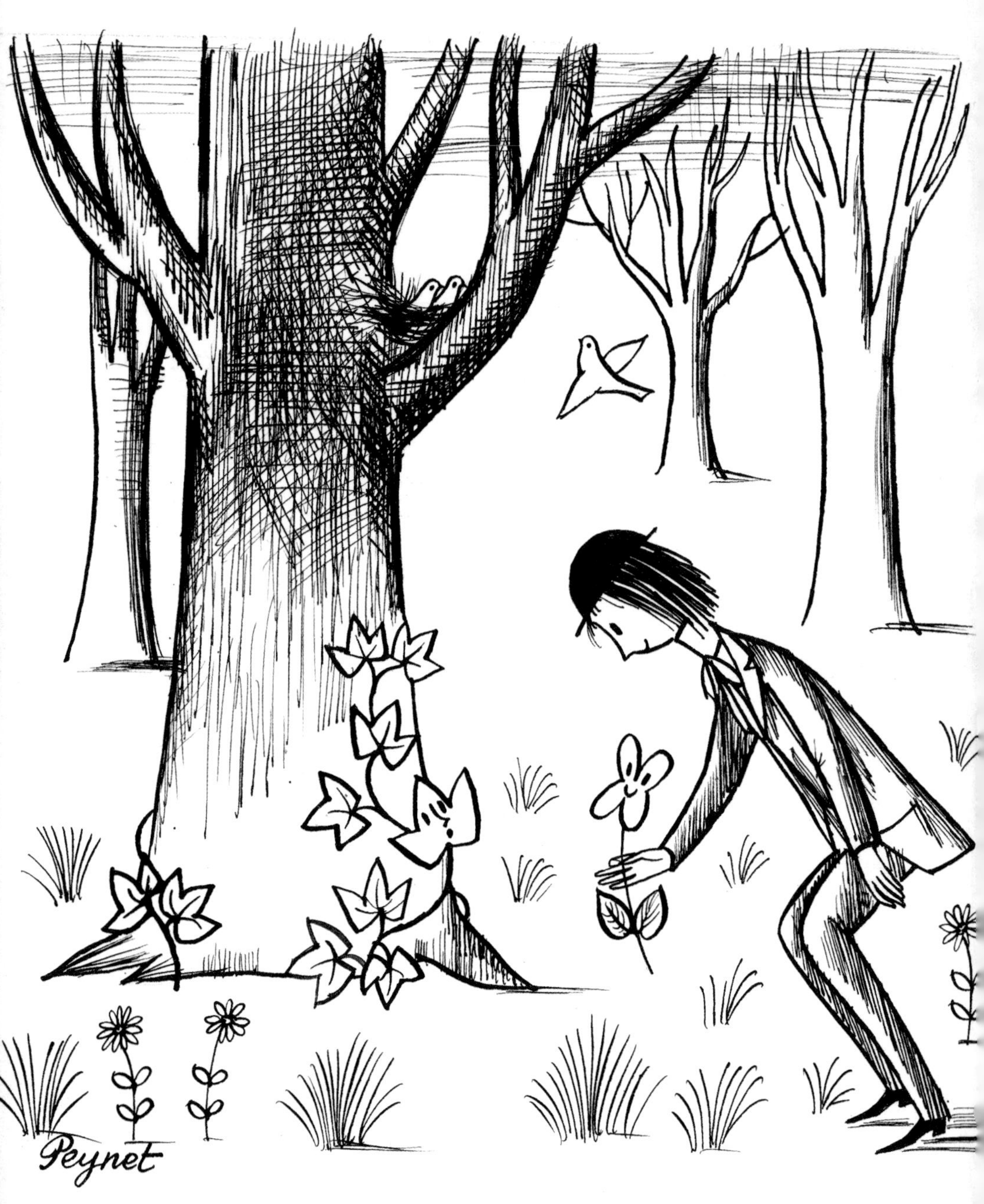
Peynet

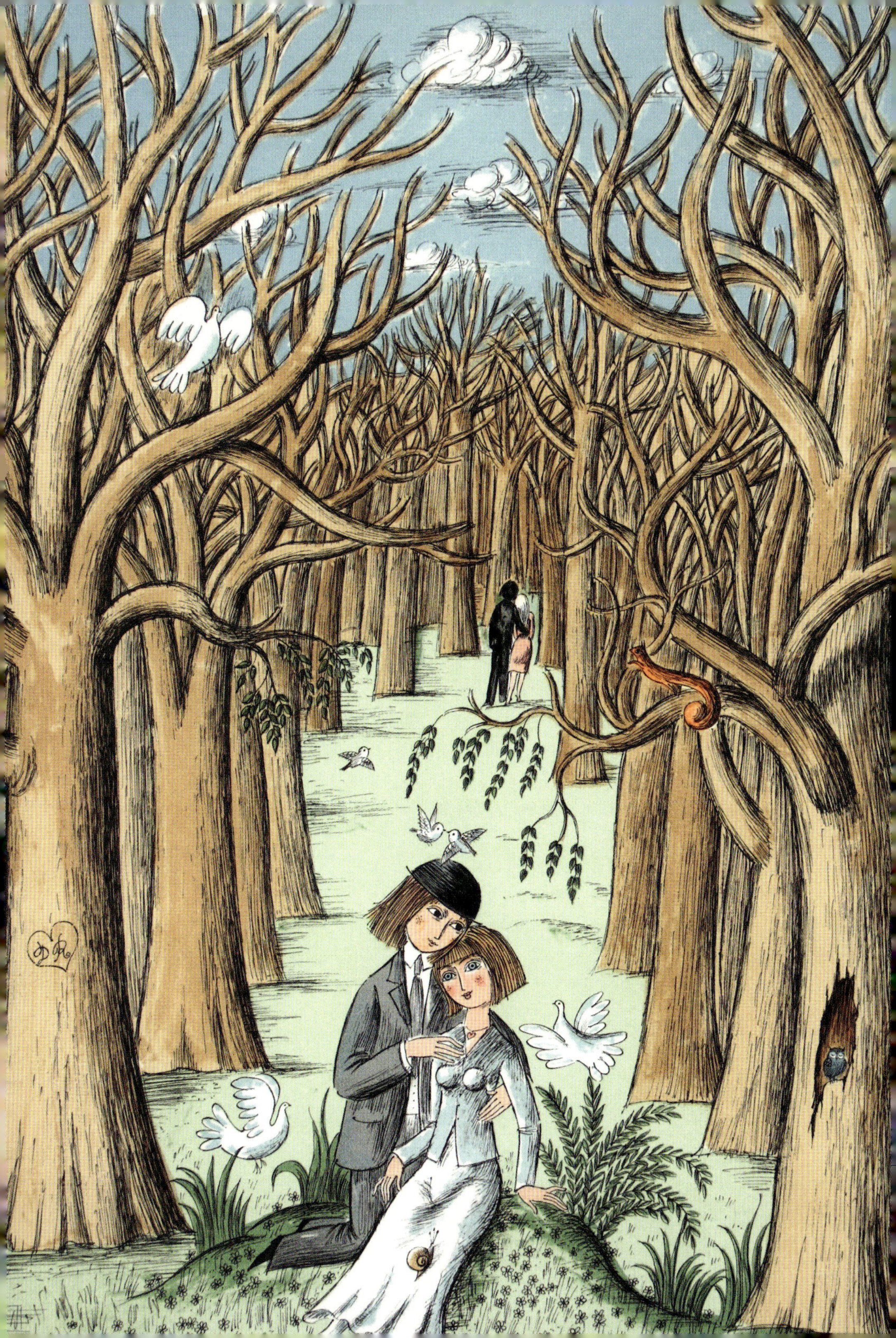

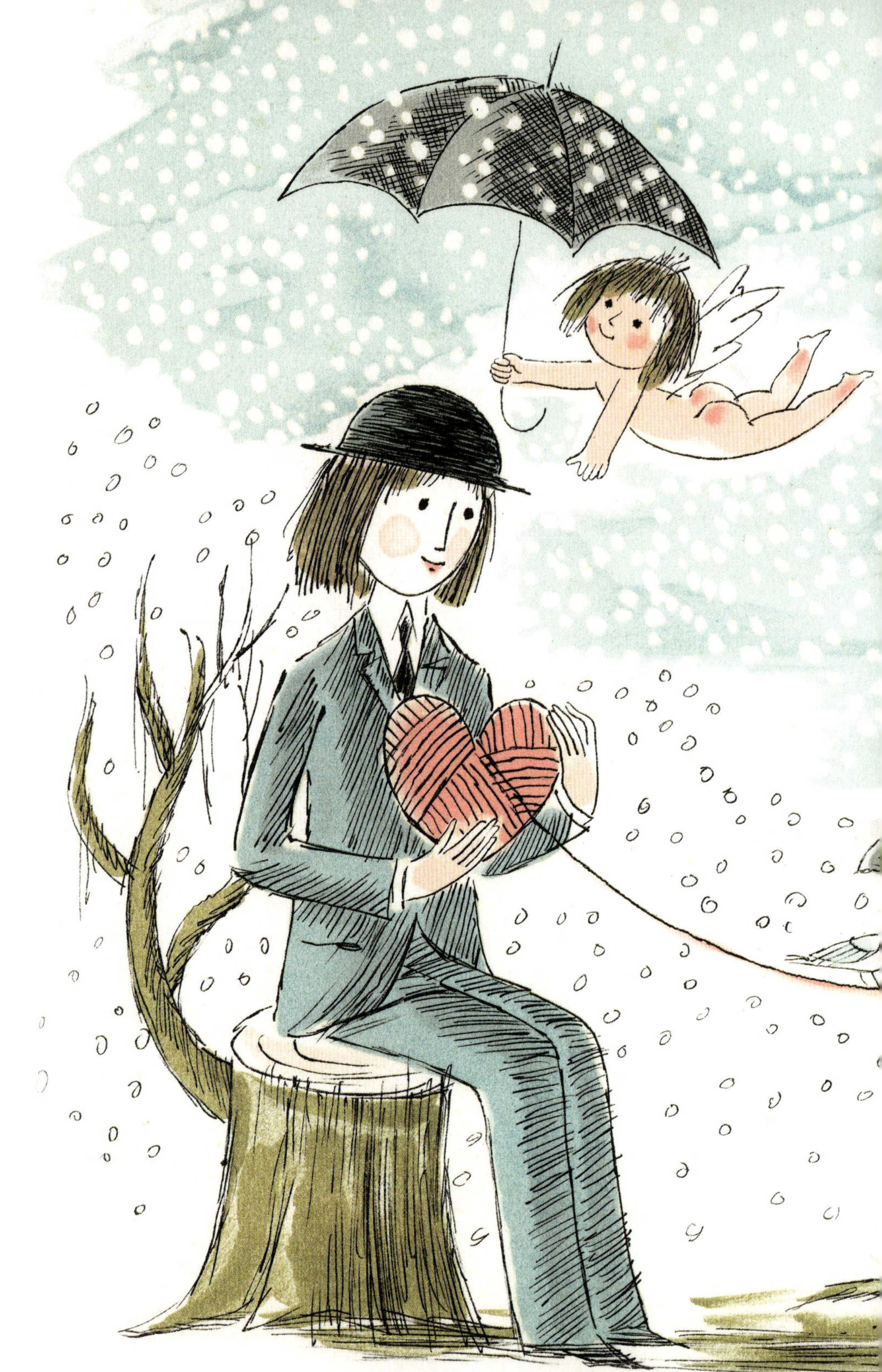

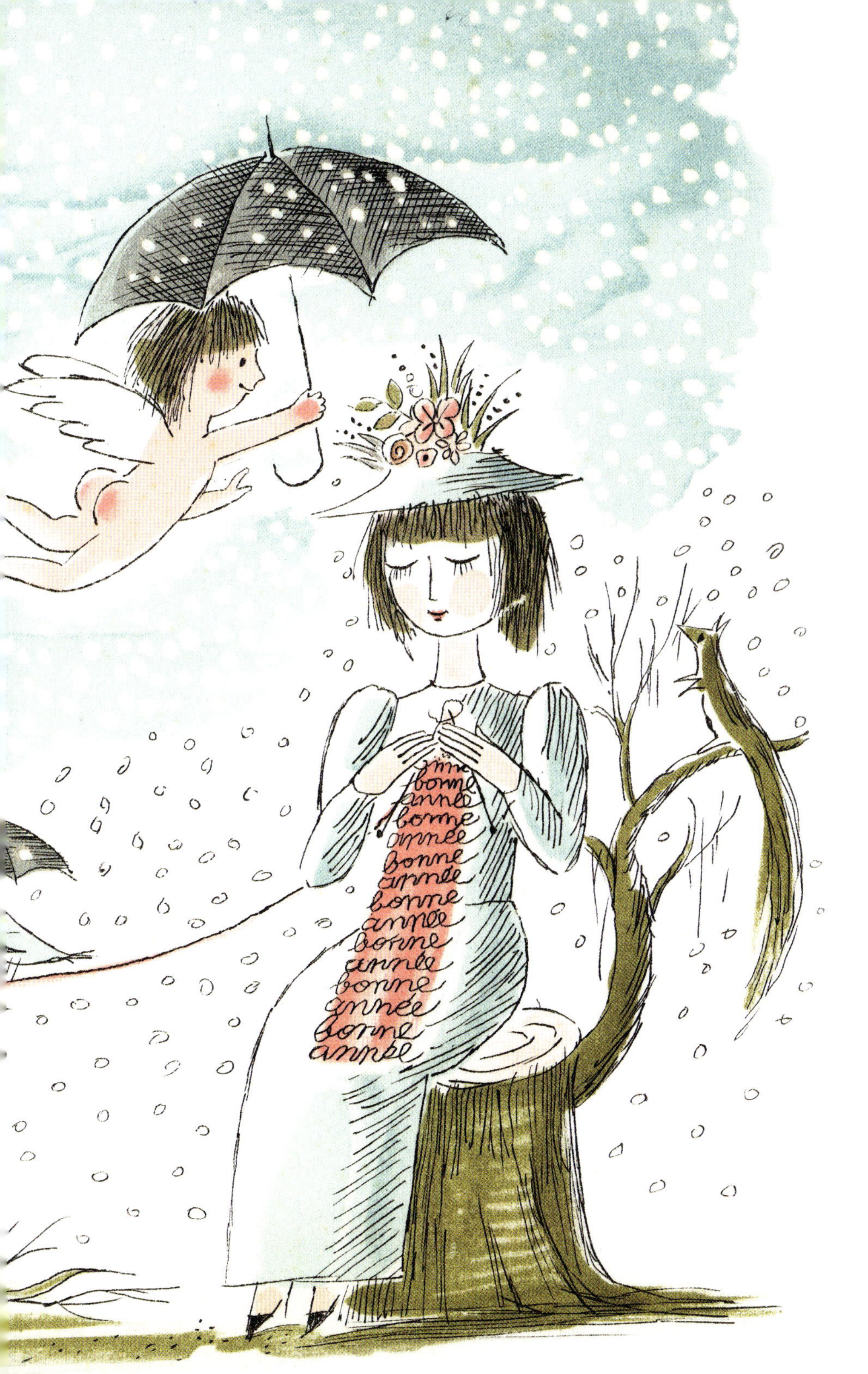
bonne
année
bonne
année
bonne
année
bonne
année
bonne
année
bonne
année
bonne
année

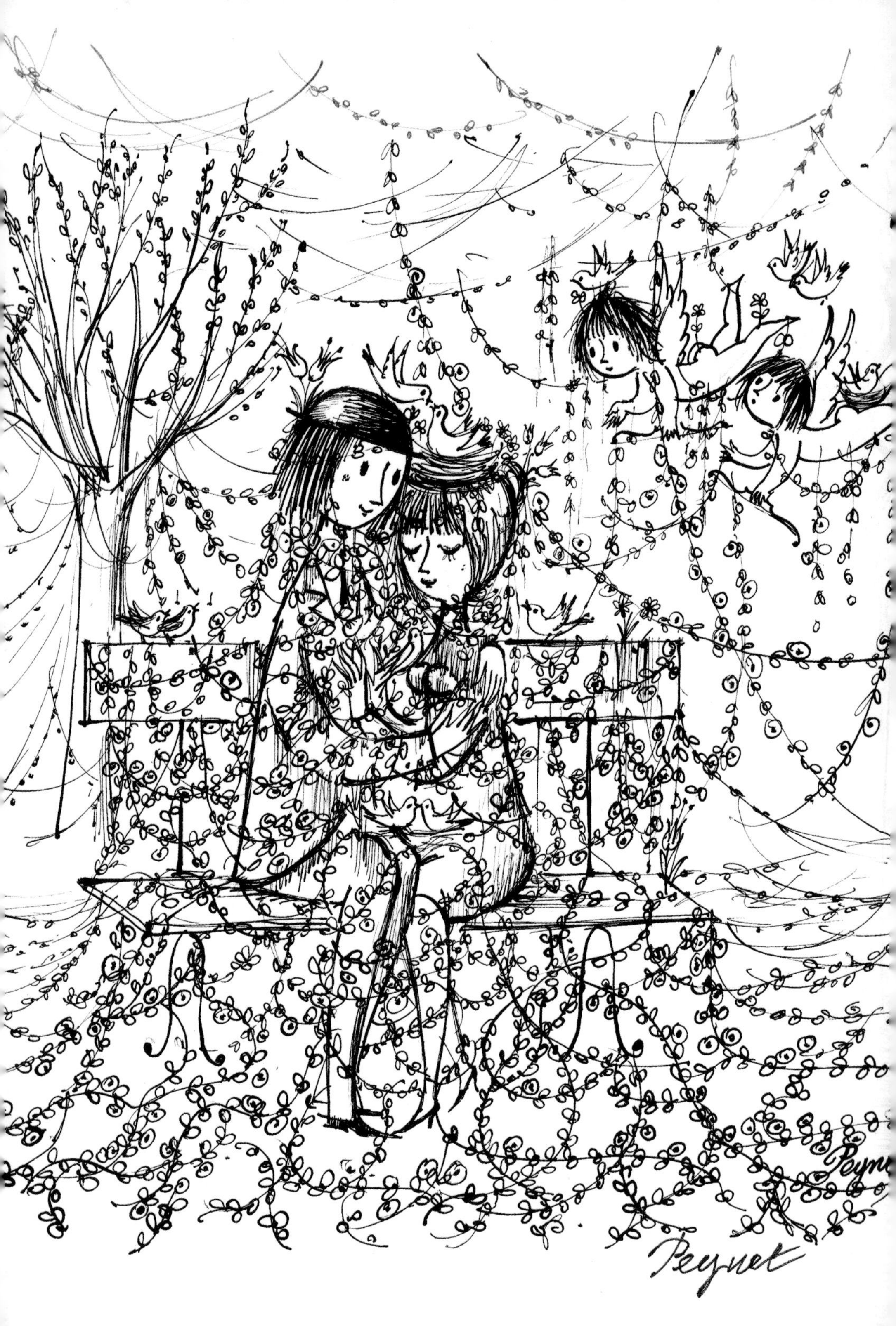
Peynet

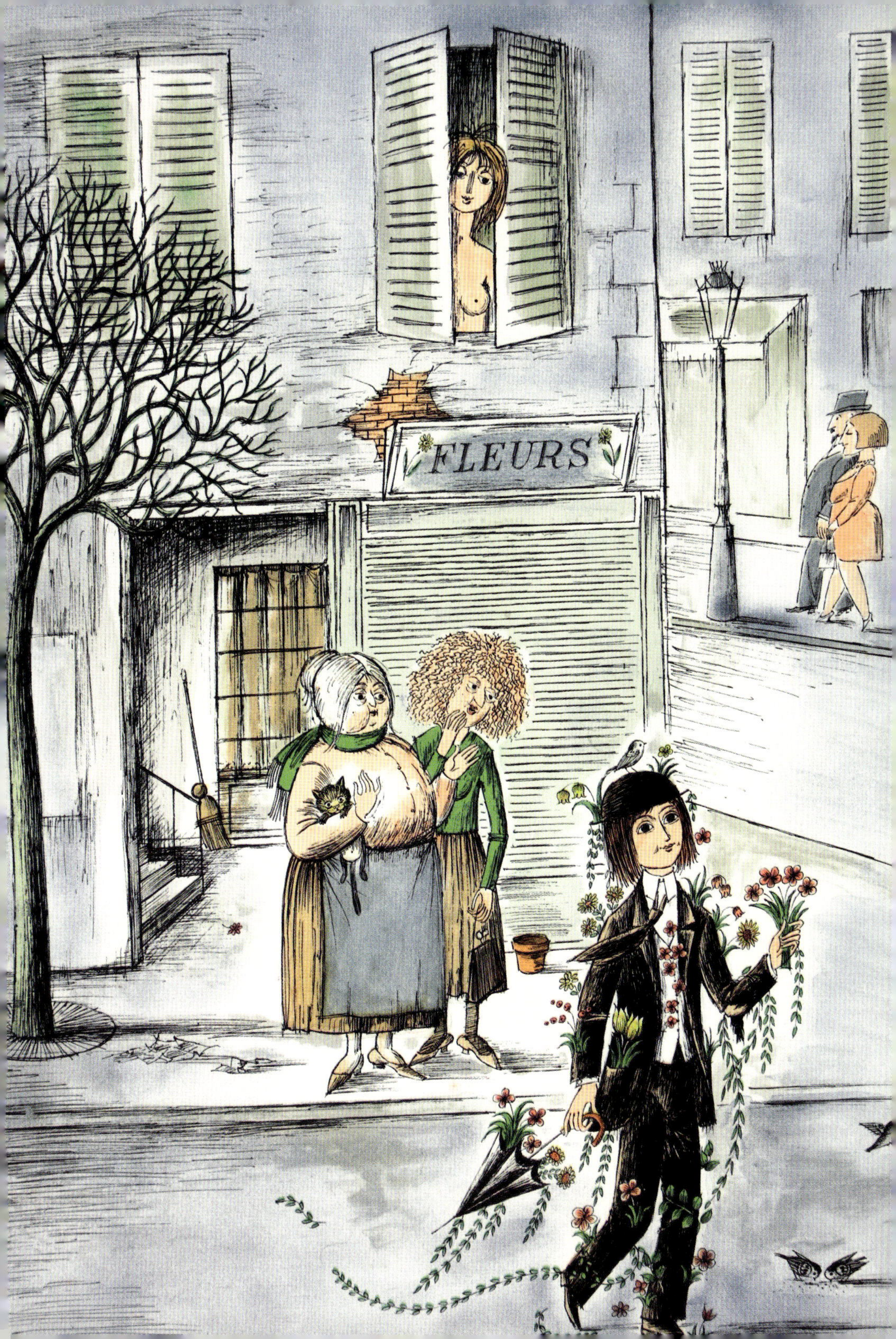
FLEURS

If love caused only sorrow, why, then, do lovebirds sing?

PHILIPPE QUINAULT
Armide

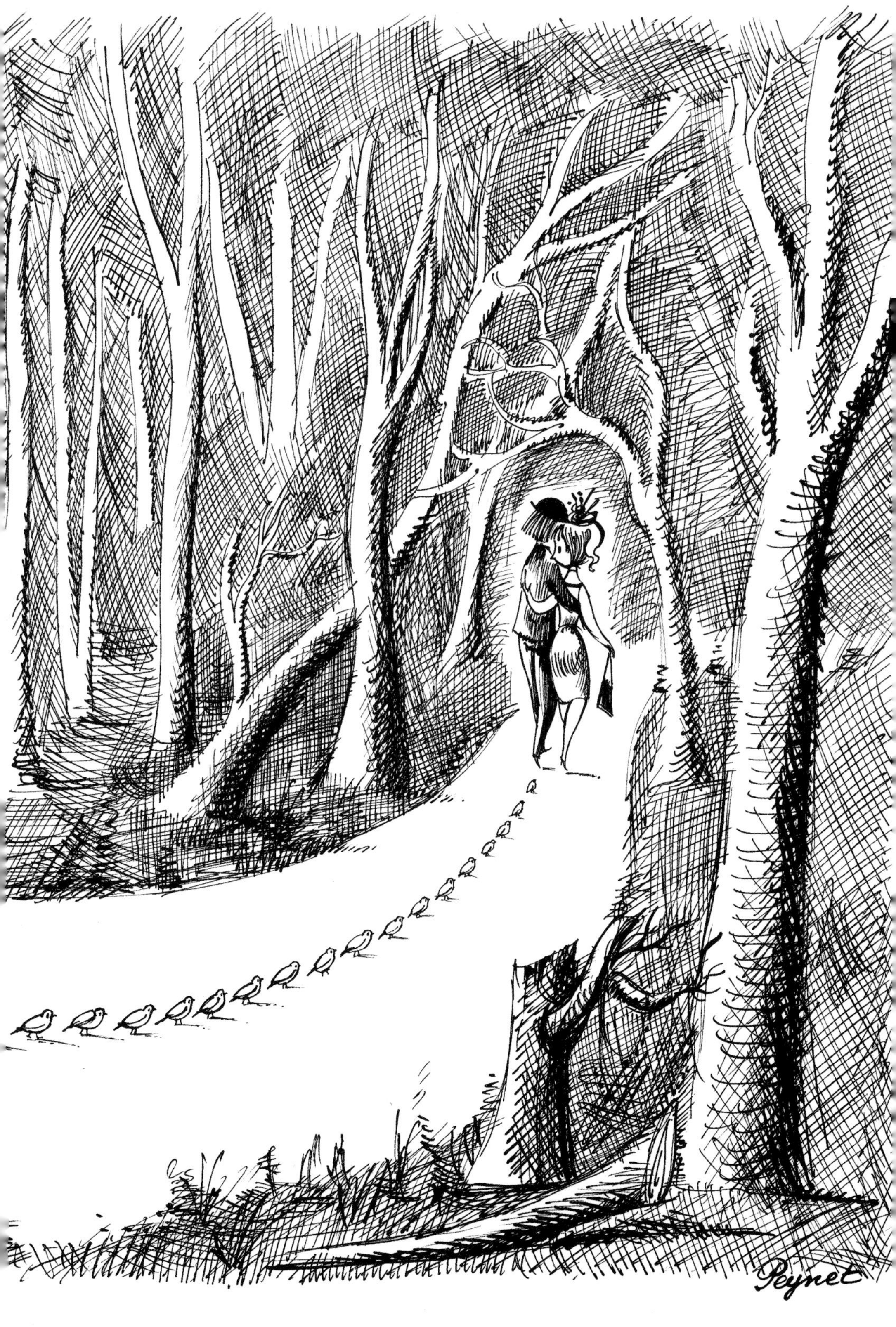
Peynet

Captions & Comments

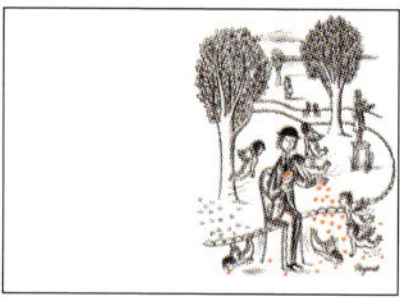

(Untitled). Pen and ink drawing, 1957.

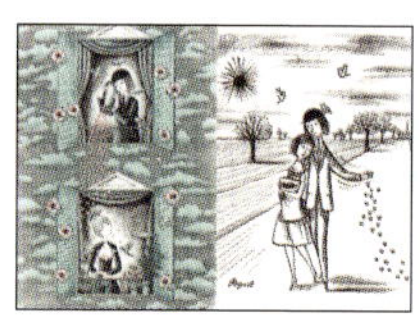

The Signs of the Zodiac: Aquarius. Etching and aquatint engraved on copper, 1979.
"We Will Sow Our Love . . ." Pen and ink drawing, 1956.

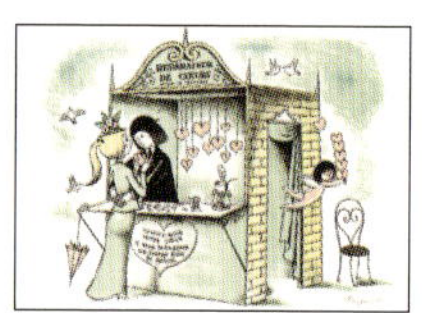

Expert Heart Repair—Shop With Confidence. Lithograph, 1975.

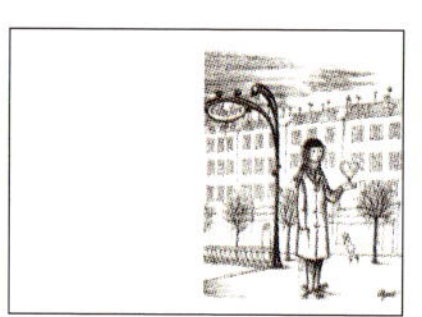

The Bashful Lover. Pen and ink drawing, 1955.

"It Is Becoming Increasingly Difficult to Find Housing Befitting a Great Love . . ." Pen and ink drawing, 1954.
The Tree of Love. Gouache, 1976.

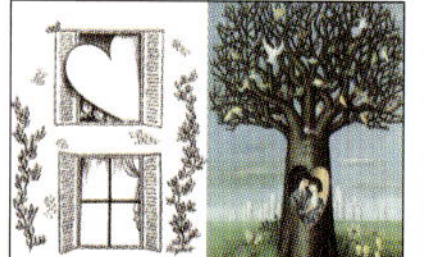

"In this drawing, the tree is a cocoon for the lovers. Peynet used pastel and gouache to represent the modern world, one quite different from the world of love. It's a strange world indeed (the magnificent intertwining and embracing branches, birds everywhere, a turtle-shaped vase filled with flowers, a small lizard whose long tail ends in a flower), and in this lovely ode to love, you completely miss the fact that the young man is fondling his girlfriend." PLANTU

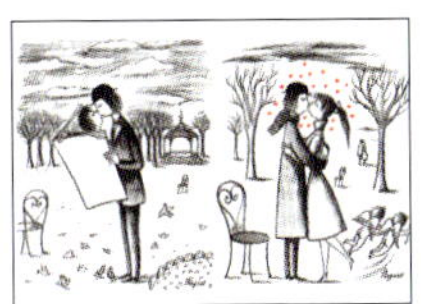

Personals. Pen and ink drawing, 1951.
"In Overtime . . ." Pen and ink drawing, 1950.
"This drawing brings to mind the posters of the 1950s, where stylized characters stand mouth to mouth, forming one single body; it's also reminiscent of Raymond Savignac's graphics." PLANTU

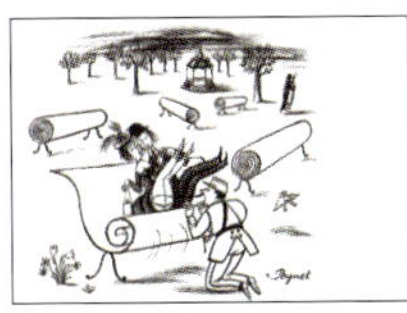

"It's 9:30, Closing Time! . . ." Pen and ink drawing, 1949.

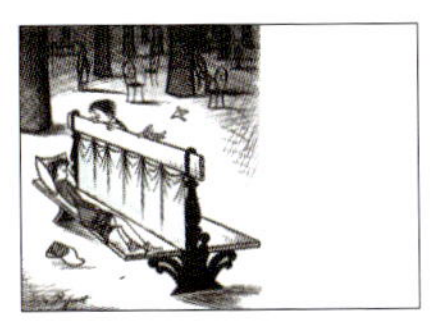

"Are You Still Angry, Honey? . . ." Pen and ink drawing, 1952.

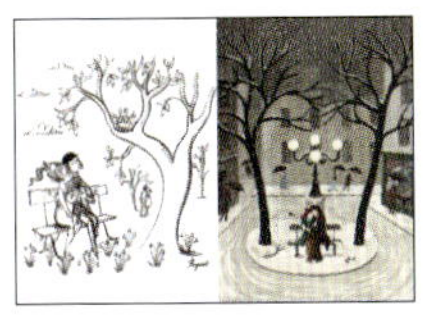

"Don't You Agree? Our Hearts Were Made for Each Other . . ." Pen and ink drawing, 1960.
Winter: "You Will Catch My Flu . . . I Will Catch Your Bronchitis . . . We'll Share the Same Medication . . ." Lithograph, 1979.
"Peynet depicts a Christmas tableau: While passersby go about their business, a couple is shielded by trees that form an honor guard around them, a natural shelter." PLANTU

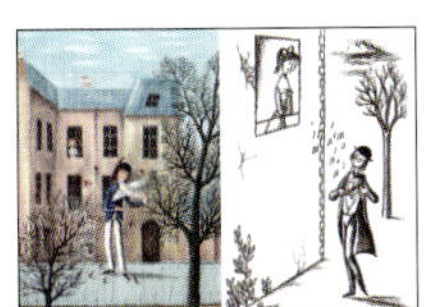

(Untitled). Gouache, 1961.
(Untitled). Pen and ink drawing, 1959.

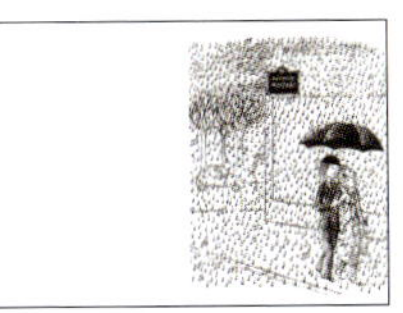

(Untitled). Pen and ink drawing, 1962.
"Everything is drawn with such a light touch, with modest, quivering, and soft strokes. The lines remind you of the filaments of life, like hair strands. The filaments become the lines of a musical score, with notes dancing along the top of the drawing; they form clouds, define the wall, and provide the sheet music for Peynet's symphony of love." PLANTU

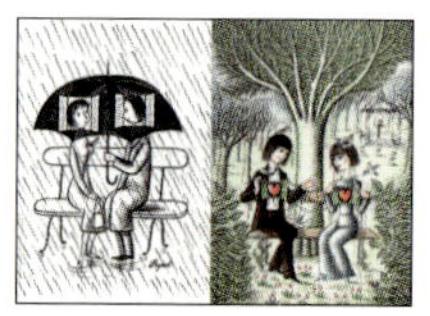

"In Such Miserable Weather, Why Not Stay Inside . . ." Pen and ink drawing, 1959.
"The lovers are sitting on a bench; a tender scene. Look again: The young woman's breasts are so appealing that a little bird has made them his perch! A well-toned bust indeed, but not the first thing you notice . . . and that's the trick!"
PLANTU

Open-Heart Surgery. Lithograph, 1979.

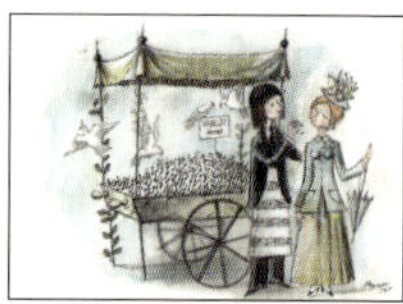

A Merchant for All (Four) Seasons. Lithograph, 1975.

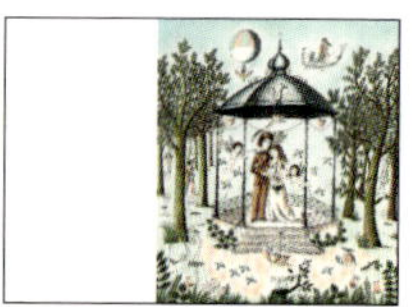

(Untitled). Lithograph, 1980.

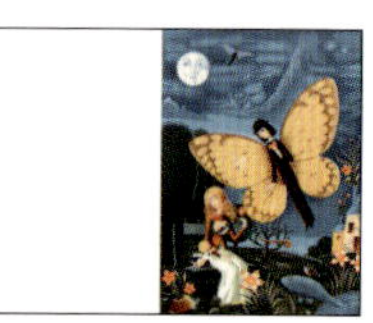

(Untitled). Lithograph, 1974.

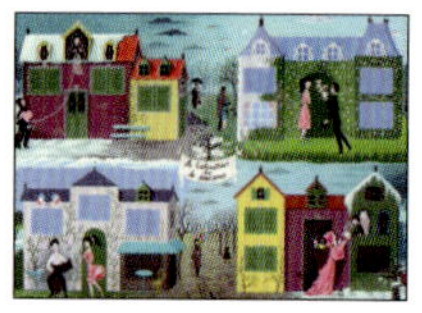

A Four Seasons Calendar. Gouache, 1962. This calendar was created for the December 1962 issue of *Elle* magazine.

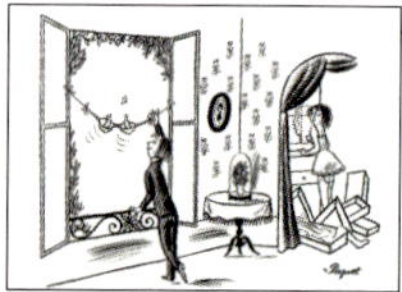

"Instead of Fooling Around, Why Don't You Help Me Look for My Brassiere! . . ." Pen and ink drawing, 1949.
"The young man has bought his lover a brassiere. We can see the old-fashioned boxes laying open on the floor. The young man would like us to believe that he has given her this brassiere to use as a nest for little birds. As if a brassiere could serve some other purpose. But that's another story." PLANTU

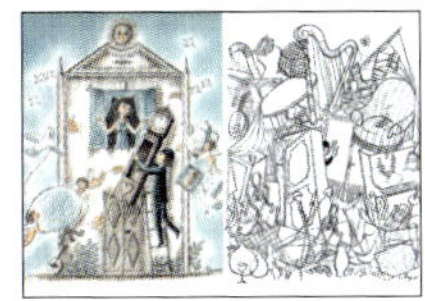

(Untitled). Gouache, 1987. This poster design was for the Salon des Antiquaires d'Antibes.
"How Much Is This Louis le Grand?" Pen and ink drawing, 1949.

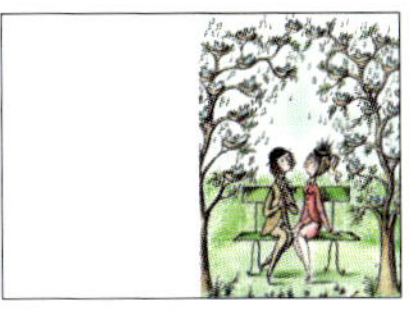

(Untitled). Lithograph, 1982.

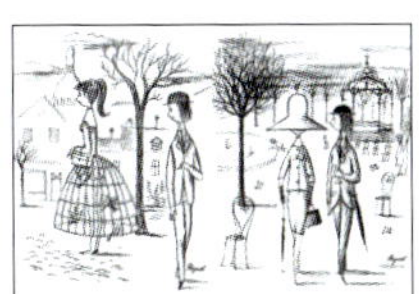

"Oh, That Reminds Me of Mimi Pinson . . ." Pen and ink drawing, 1965.
"You're Still Cross With Me! . . ." Pen and ink drawing, 1968.
"The trick here is the cloche hat, reminiscent of Audrey Hepburn in Breakfast at Tiffany's. *Peynet expresses his disapproval of the latest fashion, which hides the woman's face, by eagerly turning his attention to the sway of her hips and the way she moves. Had he seen her face, he might not have looked at her legs."* PLANTU

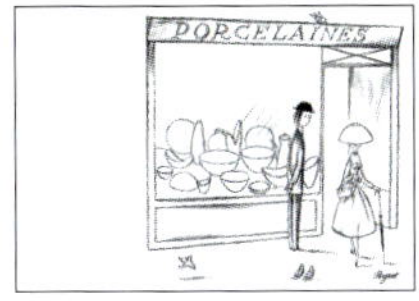

(Untitled). Pen and ink drawing, 1955.

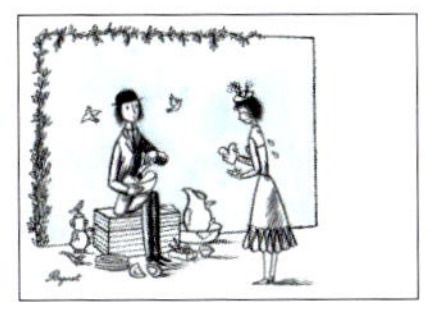

(Untitled). Pen and ink drawing, 1957.

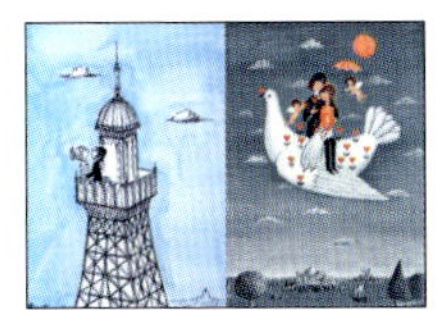

"I've Heard of Seventh Heaven. Do We Still Have Far to Go, Honey? . . ." Pen and ink drawing, 1956.
(Untitled). Lithograph, 1975.

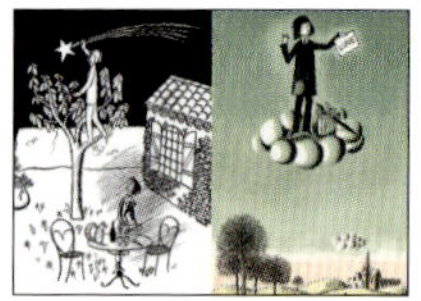

"Hand Me a Flashlight. I Can't See . . ." Pen and ink drawing, 1950.
(Untitled). Pen and ink drawing, 1974.

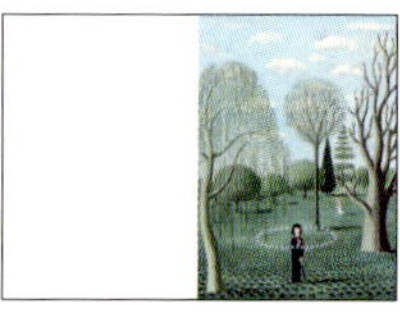

(Untitled). Gouache, 1974.

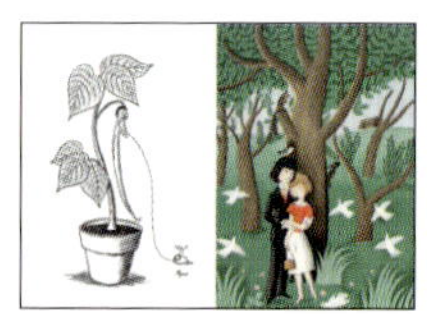

"The Vilmorin Diet Is Wonderful! Within Two Weeks, I Looked Like a String Bean . . ." Pen and ink drawing, 1955.
(Untitled). Lithograph, 1975.

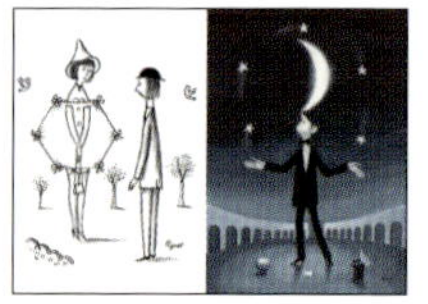

"I Heard That Yves Saint Laurent Was Designing a Hexagon Dress . . ." Pen and ink drawing, 1958.
"Peynet was a man of his time and aware of society's interest in the latest fashion trends. In this drawing, he salutes Yves Saint Laurent while still showing his acerbic side: Once the dress—which is not that pretty after all—is removed, the real gift is revealed." PLANTU
(Untitled). Gouache, 1975.

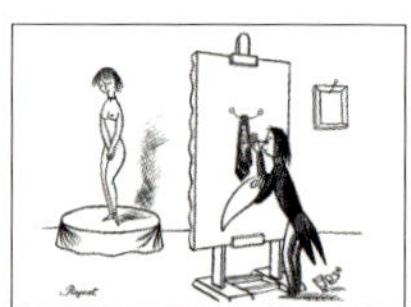

(Untitled). Pen and ink drawing, 1950.

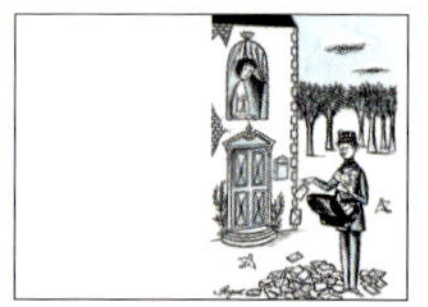

The Mailman's Route: "She Loves Me, She Loves Me Not . . ." Pen and ink drawing, 1951.

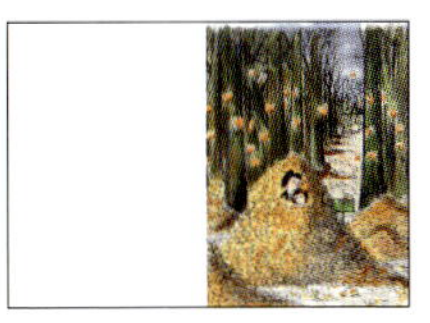

"Are You Cold, Sweetheart? No, I Am All Covered Up . . ." Lithograph, 1979.
"The falling leaves covering the lovers are drawn by pen, individually—a series of measured lines. You can almost hear the sound of the pen scratching against the high-quality paper as it catches the grain. Peynet took the time to draw the leaves the way they fall, one by one." PLANTU

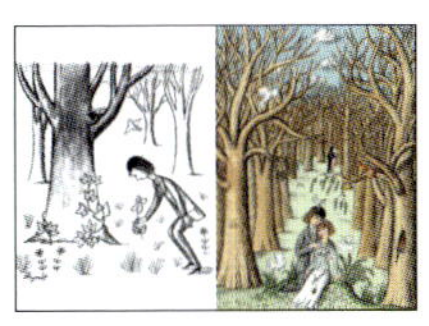

"IVY: 'He Is a Florist.' VIOLET: 'No, Not a Florist. I Think He Is a Poet. He Has Such a Gentle Touch . . .'" Pen and ink drawing, 1956.
"What Game Shall We Play: 'He Loves Me, He Loves Me Not,' 'Steal My Heart,' or 'Itsy Bitsy Spider'?" Lithograph, 1980.

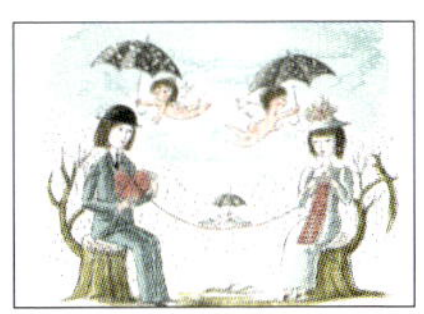

(Untitled). Lithograph for a greeting card.

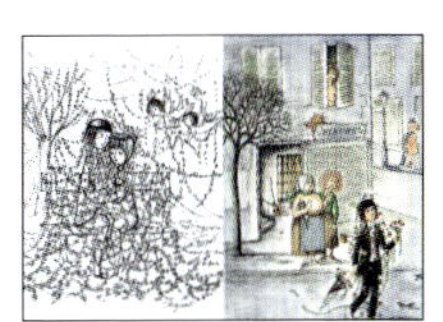

"I Can't Remember a More Fertile Spring . . ." Pen and ink drawing, 1960.
"There are birds everywhere. The young woman's eyelashes, as she looks down demurely, remind us of birds—two little doves—walking briskly. Even her mouth could be part of a dove." PLANTU
"Well, Well, the Poet Has Spent the Night with the Florist . . ." Lithograph, 1980.

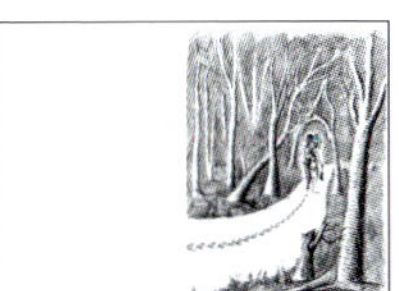

(Untitled). Pen and ink drawing, 1959.
"Lovers, seen from behind, walk innocently through the forest. We notice the young woman's body because her buttocks are shaded in gray pencil strokes, the same strokes Peynet uses to draw the forest. This is his way of saying: 'Look at these buttocks! It's not by chance that I am showing them to you, as I have used these brushstrokes throughout the drawing.'" PLANTU

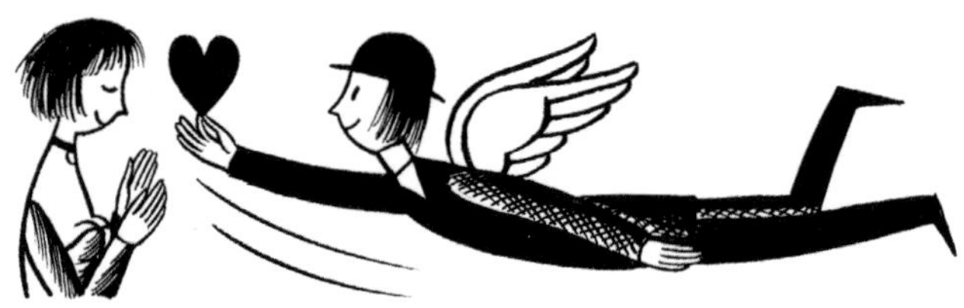

Acknowledgments

The publishers wish to thank warmly the Peynet's family.
Our thanks also to Plantu for his work and insightful analysis, and to Maïté Léon, Plantu's assistant.

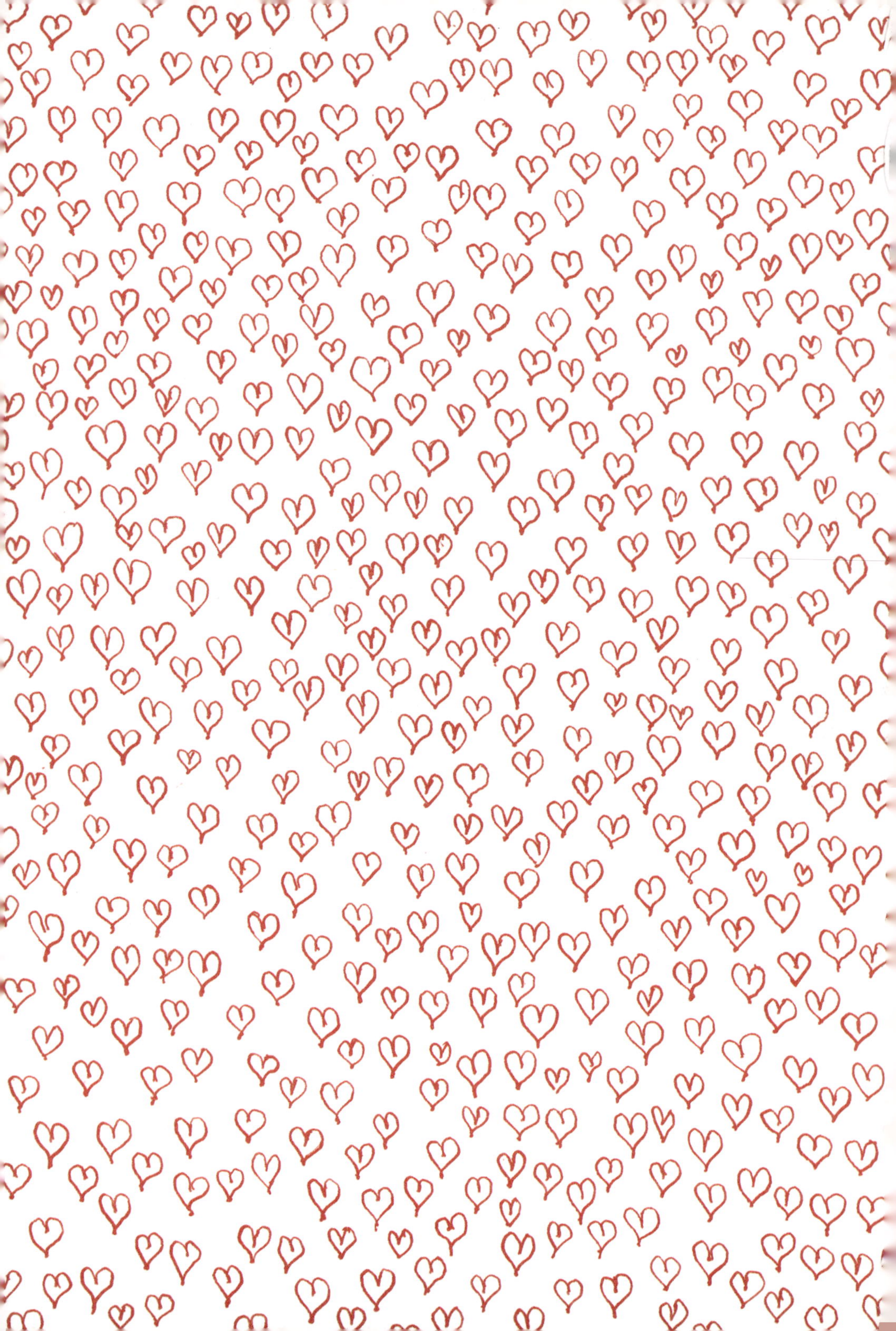